We're Czechs

NUMBER TWENTY-FIVE:
Centennial Series of the Association of Former Students,
Texas A&M University

We're Czechs

By Robert L. Skrabanek

TEXAS A&M UNIVERSITY PRESS : COLLEGE STATION

976.4
S

The paper used in this book meets the minimum requirements
of the American National Standard for Permanence
of Paper for Printed Library Materials, Z39.48-1984.
Binding materials have been chosen for durability.

Library of Congress Cataloging-in-Publication Data

Skrabanek, R. L.
    We're Czechs.

    (Centennial series of the Association of Former
Students, Texas A&M University ; no. 25)
    Bibliography: p.
    Includes index.
    1. Czech Americans—Texas—Social life and customs.
2. Farm life—Texas.   3. Texas—Social life and
customs.   I. Title.   II. Series.
F395.B67S57   1988   976.4′0049186   87-18002
ISBN 0-89096-365-7
ISBN 0-89096-413-0 pbk.

Contents

List of Illustrations   *page ix*
Preface   *xi*
Chapter 1.   The Setting   *3*
      2.   Farming—A Way of Life   *16*
      3.   Hard Work in the Fields   *46*
      4.   Close and Cooperative Relationships   *75*
      5.   Brothers and Sisters   *101*
      6.   Relatives, Friends, and Neighbors   *133*
      7.   Community Schools   *148*
      8.   School in the County Seat—
           Leaving Home   *178*
      9.   Staunch Czech Moravian Brethren   *192*
    10.   Half a Century Later   *225*
Bibliography   *231*
Index   *235*

Illustrations

The author, about 1920   *page 5*
The Skrabanek family, 1919   *6*
Members of the Snook lodge of the SPJST,
    about 1910   *12*
Dedication of Snook Czech Moravian Church, 1913   *13*
Main road of the Snook business section, early 1920s   *15*
Fourth of July celebration in Snook, about 1910   *15*
Young Snook couples canning vegetables, about 1924   *23*
Ptacek's store in Snook, 1920s   *34*
Fojt's store in Snook, about 1925   *34*
Snook Czech farmers baling hay, about 1932   *43*
A Snook lad with four mules hitched to a middlebuster plow,
    about 1934   *48*
A Snook farmer and his niece, about 1936   *51*
A Czech farmwife picking cotton, about 1933   *53*
A Czech family after emptying cotton sacks,
    about 1932   *55*
Snook cotton pickers, about 1933   *70*
The author's father and neighbor, about 1930   *73*
The Snook SPJST hall building committee, 1935   *78*
Snook Beef Club members, early 1950s   *86*
The saloon in Ptacek's store, before 1918   *100*
A Snook Czech couple and their early-1920s Model T Ford,
    about 1925   *102*
Young Snook men with a 1925 Model T coupé,
    about 1928   *104*

Two young men in front of Fojt's store in Snook,
about 1922   *106*
A buggy and the gasoline pump in front of Fojt's store,
about 1923   *110*
Wagons loaded with cotton at Fojt's gin in Snook,
about 1923   *127*
Cotton samples at Fojt's gin, about 1936   *127*
Snook SPJST hall, about 1940   *129*
The Model A Ford owned by the author's Uncle Joe,
about 1934   *137*
Young Snook adults on a trip, about 1930   *141*
The Fojt and Ptacek homes in Snook, about 1925   *142*
Two of the author's playmates and their female friend,
about 1922   *144*
The family's first painted house, about 1947   *152*
Merle School, in Snook, 1925–26 school year   *154*
Room two in Moravia School, in Snook,
1928–29 school year   *165*
The drinking-water system at Moravia School,
about 1928   *168*
Moravia School's basketball team, 1928–29   *172*
Moravia School's first girls' basketball team, about 1918   *173*
Pages from the Czech Moravian Brethren Church catechism
used in 1933   *196–97*
The 1933 confirmation class of the Snook Czech Moravian
Brethren Church   *199*
Sunday school lesson card for October 1, 1937   *202*
The Snook business section, 1948   *226*

Preface

This book is about who we were, how we lived, and the kinds of things we did when I was growing up in the 1920s and 1930s in Snook, a rural Czech community in Central Texas.

It has been my privilege to have seen many changes and to reflect on how being brought up in an all-Czech community influenced and shaped the lives of my cohorts. My birth date was one week after the World War I Armistice was signed, and my mother was said to have remarked that she was glad she had a son who would never have to live in a time of war.

There was no way my mother could have foreseen the vast changes that would unfold in my lifetime. There was no electricity in my home community when I was born. Wood-burning stoves and potbellied heaters were our only means of cooking and heating. There were no hard-surface roads in the entire county. We got our water, one bucket at a time, from a well, cistern, creek, or stock tank. One-row equipment pulled by mules followed by man on foot were a way of agricultural life. Parents and children alike were fully occupied doing things that contributed to their family's general welfare. Czech was the predominant language used in conversations and community meetings. Sunday school and church services were in Czech.

Our families were large and close-knit, and we cared for and depended on each other. Caring and a feeling of closeness extended to even the most distant relative. Divorces were unheard of. Houses were never locked, even if we were away for a few days. People were reliable and honest, and could be trusted. And heaven help the person who was judged to have come up short in any of these qualities. Parents were in full charge of deciding what was proper behavior for children, and we did not dare question their decisions.

There are lots of books that describe life and living in the early 1900s. The main thing that sets this one apart from the others is that the setting is an all-Czech rural community where we went to great lengths to preserve our Czech cultural heritage. As children we were constantly reminded of this fact by a common expression: "We're Czechs; they're Americans." But the term "Americans" didn't include all people who were of non-Czech heritage. Those who were of German extraction were "Germans." Persons of Italian ancestry were "Italians," Hispanics were "Mexicans," and blacks were "Negroes." Thus "Americans" included only those people who were of English, Scottish, or Irish ancestry and who lived on relatively small farms near our all-Czech community.

Although it was never openly stated, the expression "We're Czechs; they're Americans" clearly implied that we were privileged to be of Czech extraction and that somehow or other we were better than the Americans with whom we associated.

Some of the things described in this work may be similar, at least to some degree, to what took place in other rural communities in the 1920s and 1930s. But each ethnic group has its own special heritage, and each community its own special ways of dealing with life. It is for this reason that I wanted to describe what growing up in a Czech rural community in Central Texas was like when I was a youth.

All the things described in this book are true, or as true as they can be, based on my best recollections. Many people, especially my sister and brother-in-law Clara and Charlie Orsak, supplied information that supplemented or verified my recollections. Other lifetime residents of the Snook community, including Ella Orsak, Ed Ptacek, John Fojt, Frank Fojt, Bertha Fojt, Jerry Slovacek, Fannie C. Maresh, and Ed Mikeska, helped me clarify some of the details of incidents which happened half a century ago.

I am indebted to several fellow faculty members at Texas A&M University, including Richard Floyd, Jerry Gaston, and Steve Murdock, for their encouragement, and to John McNeely and Barbara and Pat Wooten, who served as critics. Special debts of gratitude go to my wife, Kathryn Ann Skrabanek, for her understanding and encouragement during the writing of this book.

Some of the materials in this book have appeared in other forms in my previous writings. These are listed in the Bibliography. Some of the Czech words are not precisely as they are found in a Czech dictionary but are in the form in which they were used in the Snook community in the 1920s and 1930s. I am indebted to Clinton J. Machann and Joseph J. Skrivanek, Jr., for their assistance in translation, Czech spellings, and diacritical markings.

We're Czechs

1.

The Setting

This book is about how things were when I was growing up in Snook, a rural Czech community in Central Texas in the 1920s and 1930s.

Papa (*otec* or *tatínek*) and Mama (*matka* or *maminka*) and all five of their children were born in Texas, but the way we did things in my boyhood days in many ways had a strong Czech flavor. Even though some fifty years had passed between the time my grandparents arrived in America and the date of my birth, I grew up in a situation which was like having one foot in this country with the other still in the Old Country. The reason for this was that we lived mostly among Czechs and had a much closer relationship with them than with other Americans, and I was born and reared in an all-Czech community.

"We're Czechs; they're Americans" ("My jsme Češi; oni jsou Američané") was an expression commonly used in our homes as well as in daily conversations. This expression had a lasting impression on us youngsters. But "We're Czechs; they're Americans" was not necessarily the complete phrase, because often it was accentuated with the additional admonition — "and don't you forget it!" Even if the additional words were not spoken, the tone in which they were said made it clear that they were intended to be there.

The statement "We're Czechs; they're Americans" always caught my attention, but especially when it was made in the booming voice of my father, respectfully known by all of my family members, including his wife, as Papa. Never once in my entire lifetime did I hear any of our family members refer to him as Dad, Daddy, Father, or any term other than Papa, and this included all of his grandchildren. Within the community, he was known by everyone but his relatives and closest friends as Mr. John, and this included some men and women who were his own age. Papa was the no-nonsense, business-like, uncontested head of our household. On the other hand, Mama had a gentle disposition and did not need to use forceful language, because her children would have done anything she wanted without having to be reminded of our heritage. Unlike Papa, she was called Grandma by her grandchildren, Mrs. Frances by most of the community residents, and Frances by her closest friends.

The expression "We're Czechs; they're Americans" seemed somehow or other to give the impression to us kids that we were a cut above the other white people who spoke English only and lived on small farms near our community. But in what way this was true was never clearly spelled out. Even though the phrase was used frequently, it had its most lasting impression on us when one of us, perhaps in a moment of either forgetfulness or just pure daring, worked up enough courage to raise a question about something Papa had decreed should be done. One such example clearly stands out in my memory.

I was about eight years old at the time, the fifth child and the baby of the family. All of our family members were seated at the table eating supper (no one ever ate or even tasted food before all family members were present and properly seated). All of us were in our designated places (there also was none of this business of sitting just any place anyone might feel like). Papa sat at the head of the long rectangular table; Mama at the opposite end closest to the kitchen so she could get something during the meal if it was needed; my two brothers, Henry and Johnnie, and I on one side on a homemade bench; and my two sisters, Ella and Clara, on the opposite side. The girls shared a bench, but Papa and Mama rated chairs. These did

The author, about 1920, beside the house in which he was born and lived until he moved with his family to another farm in 1926. His homemade clothes were called "rompers" and were made from a flour or sugar sack. They buttoned down the back and had a flap that could be unbuttoned for visits to the outhouse.

The Skrabanek family journeyed to Bryan for this pose in 1919. FRONT, LEFT TO RIGHT: Clara, Johnnie. MIDDLE: John (Papa), Robert (the author), Frances (Mama). TOP: Henry, Ella. (Photograph courtesy Bertha Fojt)

not match, but everybody knew which one was Papa's and which was Mama's.

Right in the middle of the usual warm and friendly banter which led to occasional outbursts of laughter and friendly comments, on this particular occasion, Papa announced in his usual firm voice:

"Tomorrow morning, we're going to chop the weeds in the cornfield. They're growing so big that anybody going by on the road can see them and will think we're not taking as good care of our land as we ought to." This pronouncement brought an abrupt halt to all conversation. Suddenly, my middle brother, Johnnie, who really did not expect his suggestion to be accepted because, after all, Papa had spoken, got up enough courage to say something. In a hesitant tone of voice, he ventured a trial balloon.

"Papa," he posed, "Tommy Davis's daddy said they weren't going to chop weeds in their corn since the crop is already made. And the weeds will be plowed under soon anyway." Sensing that he should not have spoken, but encouraged by not getting an immediate response, he ventured a follow-up statement as an attempt to at least lessen the amount of work:

"The Joneses chopped their weeds, but only as far as people can see from the road. And they let the weeds grow on the lower end."

Before anyone could say anything else, Papa's sharp and firm response was: "Well, that's just like those Americans — they always look for ways to get out of work. We don't do things that way. We're Czechs; they're Americans!" Thus Papa had spoken, and we knew that his decision was final and irrevocable.

Although we kids may have done some grumbling privately about having to chop weeds when the American kids did not have to, it never was within earshot of either Mama or Papa. Instinctively, we knew Mama sympathized with us, but she would never let us know it or that she ever disagreed with any decision Papa made, much less this one. Even though we may have groused a little, we really did not resent Papa's edict too much, because we knew he was not sentencing us kids to doing time in the corn patch just for the heck of it. For all of his outward sternness and dictatorial characteristics, underneath it all was a compassionate person who just felt it was important to have a clean field. And besides, it would be good for his children to have a good workout with a hoe — it would be another good character-building experience.

As it turned out, the task was not so bad. The next morning we had all our chores done and breakfast over extra-early. All five of us kids and Mama and Papa were in the field chopping weeds before we could see the first part of the sun coming up.

As the sun began to climb, the conversations became more lively and cheerful. Papa always was the pacesetter. Being the youngest, whenever I got too far behind, he worked extra-fast and chopped on my row along with his so I could catch up with the rest.

In more sober moments, I felt good about the neat rows of bright-green corn against the black, waxy soil, blended in with the slain weeds that lay wilting in the bright sun. And everyone would see that our land was better cared for than the Americans'!

The cornfield was only about five acres, and we completed the job by midafternoon. By the time we had finished, everyone was in a good mood, and especially so when Papa declared that if a stranger went by on the road he would know the field belonged to Czechs. And he added to our pleasure by announcing we would make a freezer of ice cream after supper because we all did such a good job.

I still remember, sixty years later, how good that home-made ice cream tasted — a taste that no commercial manufacturer has ever come close to matching within my lifetime.

The frequent reminders that we were Czechs had a lasting influence on the youngsters who grew up in my home community. Even today I find myself automatically explaining to people I meet for the first time that my last name is of Czech origin, a practice not commonly followed by persons of other ethnic derivations. We are very proud of our Czech heritage, having come by it naturally, since this is something that has been carefully nurtured through the generations.

The Czechs are a Slavic people who lived mainly in Moravia and Bohemia — today two provinces in Czechoslovakia — since the fifth century. Their native land had no outlet to the sea, and they were constantly overrun by marauding groups, who imposed their own languages and political and religious views on them. The many years of frustrations, and at times utter despair, in having to adjust to the harsh demands of the frequently changing regimes are illustrated by the title of the official Czech national anthem, "Kde Domov Můj ?" The literal translation of this title is "Where Is My Home?"

By the middle part of the nineteenth century, the Czechs were convinced that emigration was better than living in poverty, being persecuted for their religious beliefs, and having their language and culture suppressed. Some were among the early settlers who came to our nation's eastern shore, but the big wave of immigration to Texas occurred during the second half of the nineteenth century and consisted mainly of peasants who came with the intention of eventually buying farmland and settling permanently, breaking completely away from their native land.

The first groups came through the port of Galveston and poured into Austin County, approximately one hundred miles northwest of Galveston, where they formed the first real Czech settlement in the state at Cat Spring in 1847. After becoming acclimated to the new country, they spread out in a fairly steady migration flow, first to adjoining counties and then successively to others, but remaining especially within the Blackland Prairie Soil Region of Texas. This narrow strip of fertile blackland soils runs north and south from Galveston to just north of Dallas. This pattern was directly related to the search for good farmland at a reasonable price, a factor that led to their eventual settlement in Burleson County and particularly the area about thirty miles north of Cat Spring that later became the Snook community.

By 1880, the principal Czech communities in Burleson County were Nový Tábor (later Americanized and changed to New Tabor) and Caldwell. The latter community especially had attracted a large number of Czechs. In the New World, these people were closely bound together and tried to help each other on every possible occasion. The Czechs in Caldwell found out that some Americans were of the opinion that the pockets of black, waxy soil they owned in Burleson County were not very suitable for their purposes. Therefore, they were willing to sell the land at a comparatively low price. The Caldwell Czechs got in touch with Czechs in surrounding counties and suggested that they might want to take advantage of this particular opportunity.

One of the first Czech families to live on land in what later was to become the Snook community bought approximately 120 acres. They were the Josef Slovacek family. A son, who had immigrated with his parents to the United States and was living on this same land in 1948, gave me the following statement about his family's movement to the area:

> From Europe we first came to Galveston and then to Ross Prairie in Fayette County. We were farming on 37 acres we owned. But there were seven of us in the family and since the land was not very good, my father thought that we ought to move to a new place where the land was better and where we could farm more acres. So he was looking for a new place.
>
> Some Czech people in Caldwell sent word by a peddler that good blackland was available at a cheap price in Burleson County. My father went to see the land and while there bought 120 acres. As soon as he got back, we packed our belongings and started for what was to become our new home. It took us three days to cover the distance in a wagon which was pulled by mules. We arrived here on November 17, 1884. Within fourteen days after we got here, two more Czech families moved into the area. They were the Martin Kocureks and Joe Mikulas.

Seeing a chance to form an all-Czech community where they would not have to live among persons of other nationalities, the first families to arrive in what is now Snook invited other Czechs to move into the area. They also tried to discourage those who were of non-Czech origin. Within the brief span of a few years, the land was occupied by persons of their own kind, and a Czech cultural island was created where their common language, beliefs, practices, and customs could be preserved. In addition to those families previously mentioned, some of the early settlers were the Sebestas, Hurtas, Mareks, Fojts, Mikeskas, Rubaches, Vajdaks, and Kosinas.

Each new family moving into the area was heartily welcomed. Even though they were struggling to raise crops and pay off the money they had borrowed to buy land, build homes and outbuildings, and purchase livestock and equipment, they shared their labor and contributed in other ways to help the new arrivals. They lost little time in developing the community. A cooperative store was organized in the latter part of the 1880s. This apparently was the only cooperative store in the entire county and was owned and operated mutually by and for Czechs, and all records and minutes of meetings were in Czech. A local chapter of the national Czechoslovakian Benevolent Society (Česko-Slovanská Podporující Spolek) also was organized in the latter 1880s. This was a mutual life insurance organization for Czechs, which also made loans to members at low interest rates and served as a social organization. A few years later, local residents organized Lodge Slovan of the Slovanic Benevolent Society of Texas (Slovanská Podporující Jednota Státu Texas—SPJST) and built another lodge hall. In 1901, a third lodge, the Farmers' Mutual Protective Society (Rolnický Vzajemný Ochranný Spolek—RVOS) was formed to provide mutual property insurance for Czechs. The meetings and minutes of all three lodges were in the Czech language until the 1930s.

A one-room school was built in 1888 and was named Moravia School after the province from which the residents had emigrated to America.

The Czechs held Protestant religious services at first in the homes of individuals. An ordained minister was able to hold services but had to come fifty miles or more, usually from

Members of the Snook SPJST lodge at the Somerville lumberyard picking up lumber to build their hall, about 1910. (Photograph courtesy Ernest Jakubik)

Fayette, Austin, or Washington County. More frequently, however, services were held without a minister present. All of the services, including hymns, Scripture lessons, Bible readings, and announcements, were in the Czech language. In 1913, a Czech Moravian Brethren church building was constructed on land donated by a member family, and the group became affiliated with the Evangelical Unity of the Czech Moravian Brethren (Evangelické Jednoty Česko-Moravských Bratří). The Roman Catholics eventually constructed a church in 1917, Saint Jacob's Catholic Church (Katolický Chrám Pana Svatého Jakůba), just within the outer perimeter of the Snook community.

Soon after the arrival of the first Czech settlers in the blackland section of a larger area generally known as Mound Prairie, they hoped to have a name of their own for it. Al-

The local congregation and visitors at the dedication of Snook Czech Moravian Brethren Church in 1913. The congregation remained in this building until a new one was constructed on an all-weather road in 1959. (Photograph courtesy Ella Orsak)

though never accepted in an official capacity, one small part of the larger area occupied by the Czechs in the earlier years was referred to locally as Sebesta's Corner and later shortened to Sebesta. Their mailing address was a Caldwell rural route.

They thought that if they could get a post office it would have an official name, and they could be identified as a specific place of residence. How this was accomplished and how it led to the selection of the name of the community in 1895 was described to me in 1948 by one of the residents who played a major role in these incidents:

> Since we had a few business establishments and buildings concentrated in one place, we wanted our own post office, too. Our problem was to find out how we could get around the law. It [the law] stated that no two post offices could be located closer than a specified distance of each other. We knew that Dabney Hill had a post office and that it was too close to our business places for us to have one. Dabney Hill was a sandy land Negro settlement about a mile or so from the Snook business section. So we did the best thing that we could have done. The man who was postmaster at Caldwell and in charge of our rural route at that time was named John S. Snook. So we told him that if we got a post office of our own, we would name it after him. When we told him that, he went to work on it. Strangely enough, before long, the Dabney Hill post office was relocated right in our business section. And it was named Snook.

So it came about that Snook, which was an all-Czech community, was not named for one of the Czech residents as a matter of expediency. Nevertheless, they had found the answer to the question posed in the title of the national anthem of their former homeland, "Where Is My Home?" They were happy to be living in the community they had founded, which in a real sense had become their own. Here they could be themselves, perpetuate their Czech heritage, and live in a land of freedom. It was into this all-Czech rural community setting that I was born in 1918.

Part of the main road running through the business section of Snook in the early 1920s. The building on the right is Fojt's store, and Fojt's gin is at the far left. (Photograph courtesy John Fojt) BELOW: *Floats and automobile in a Fourth of July parade and celebration in Snook, about 1910, in appreciation of the freedom the Czechs found in their new country.* (Photograph courtesy Ed J. Ptacek)

2.

Farming—A Way of Life

Farming was much more than just a way of making a living in my home community in the 1920s and 1930s. It was a distinctive way of life and dominated our very existence in much the same way that mining does where the entire population derives its living from the mine. We ate, drank, and slept farming. So, it was only natural that when two or more adults got together, the main topic of conversation had something to do with agriculture. Whether or not I could plan on doing something with a friend on a Saturday largely depended on whether there was fieldwork to be done.

The Snook Czechs took great pride in owning farmland. This was a natural carryover from our Czech ancestors, who have been described in literature as a land-hungry peasantry in a country where land was at such a premium that it was almost worshiped. Success, to the Snook Czechs, meant the ownership of a farm with the necessary buildings and equipment. So strong was this particular value that even all of the owners of businesses in the community owned farmland.

Not only did the ownership of land have a high place in our system of values, but also it was to be treated with the greatest of respect. A man's worth was judged by how well his farm and everything else that goes with it were kept. A farmer who had weeds growing in his field or had a mule whose mane was permitted to grow scraggly was looked down on. In fact, he even might have been thought of as being more like one of the Americans than like one of us Czechs. On the other hand, it was something to be proud of when one was complimented on a good-looking pair of mules or was told that his land and crops looked good. So farming overshadowed everything else.

I always have felt that most writers have overromanticized the pleasures of farming and underemphasized the amount of hard work involved. Our parents thrived on hard work, and if it was good for them, it had to be good for their children. It was as if we had adopted a philosophy that hard work not only was good for the soul but was a good antidote for any and all adversity. If the price of cotton was low, then if we worked extra hard, God would reward us in other ways. One thing for sure—we did not feel the need to exercise after a full day's work in the cotton- or cornfields.

Another sure thing was that we worked a lot harder than the Americans, who not only admitted it openly but even made fun of how hard we worked. Some of it was a matter of ethnic differences—for example, their women did not work in the fields as ours did. But it also may have been partly because of the different kinds of farming we did. We were blackland dirt farmers first and had a few cattle in addition to crops. The Americans mainly had cattle and devoted less acreage to crops on their sandy land. Papa always said that this difference was basically because the Americans did not want to put out the amount of work it took to farm crops as compared to raising cattle, which required a whole lot less labor. But I often thought the answer may not have been as simple as Papa made it out to be. It may have been that dirt farming was something we naturally inherited from our European ancestors, and it may have been just as natural for the Americans to prefer livestock over dirt farming. So the different types of farming we did may not have been influenced so much by the amount of work involved. But no one could have disputed the fact that we worked a lot harder.

The amount and kinds of work to be done on our farm varied with the different seasons of the year and from one day to another. But life never was dull, because there always was enough to go around for everybody at all times. While farming has been described by some as often working from sunup to sundown, a more appropriate description for us Czechs would have been from dawn until dusk. The differences in our work habits and those of the American kids showed up in school when we started basketball or track practice. The coach did not have to spend any time getting us Czech boys in shape, while the American kids had a tough time keeping up with us.

In the spring and summer months, our day started when it was still pitch-dark. Mama and Papa were up first. Being a light sleeper, I was awakened by their muffled voices and the scraping sound of ashes being scooped out of the cookstove from the previous day's accumulation. They tore up newspapers; added kindling, a few corncobs, and wood; splashed kerosene (which we called coal oil) on it; and finally started the fire with a match. As soon as a small pot of water was heated, Papa made himself a hot toddy with which to start his day.

Having properly started the day with his toddy, Papa struck a match on the underside of the small table holding the kerosene lamp in our boys' room. He lit the lamp and turned the wick up and let us know it was time to get up and get our chores done so we could eat breakfast and be in the field before sunup. We knew Papa meant business, and a second call wasn't necessary.

It did not take but a few seconds to get our clothes on, since all we had to do was pull them over the undershorts in which we slept. (I owned my very first pair of pajamas when I was about fifteen years of age. Even then, they were not used at home but were bought for use when I stayed overnight with some American kids.)

After making a quick pass at washing our faces and hands in the water in a one-quart metal pan on a homemade stand on the back porch, we fanned out in different directions to do our early-morning chores. Most of us washed in the same water since it had to be used sparingly. Also the water always was at back-porch temperature since it would have been too much trouble to go all the way to the stove and back to get some warm water even on cold mornings.

Everybody had chores to be done before breakfast from the time we were about five years of age. Mama's job was to get breakfast and get things ready for the noon and evening meals. The girls made beds and put things in order in the house. Papa busied himself getting things ready for the field, such as sharpening hoes, repairing harness, and filling water jugs if they were to be used that day. The boys took care of such things as milking the cows and feeding the workstock and farm animals.

I did not mind getting up early and doing the before-breakfast chores, because we had been brought up to believe that each job, no matter how small, was important and that each one of us was a part of a team that worked closely together to get everything done. Walking out in the yard after a good night's sleep and a splash of water on my face was a pleasant feeling. As Mama used to say, when it was still dark was the nicest part of the day. Even in the hottest part of a Central Texas summer, the early morning air was always cool and fresh and had a clean smell to it. The beauty of it all is still a fond memory, especially when the moon was full and reflected gently on everything as far as one could see. And it was quiet. About the only sound might have been an occasional crowing of a proud rooster, the neighing of a horse or mule, or the lowing of a cow somewhere off in the distance. The chickens were coming out of the hen house, stretching and fanning slowly across the barnyard. The cows and mules were at the gates of their lots, ready to be let in to get their feed. Everything was so peaceful before we began our chores. The greedy, hungry calves strained at the gate from the inside of the lot, ready to make a charge at their mother's milk at the very first opportunity. As soon as the gate was opened, the calves attacked udders with greedy, sucking sounds which lasted only a few brief minutes until the mother cow let her milk down. The calves then were tied to a post to impatiently tug at the rope until milking was finished and they were turned loose to finish up.

As our paths crossed during our early-morning chores, friendly pleasantries were exchanged with a brother — perhaps a comment about his date the night before or something personal to be shared. He also liked to pick on me. When he was milking and I dared come within squirting distance, he pretended he was not aware of my presence until I got well within range. Suddenly, he would direct the cow's teat at me and spray me with milk. If he hit his target, he would be the winner that day. If I was fast enough to elude being hit, he would concede me a win, but always vowing to get me the next time. We also enjoyed an occasional corncob fight. The first one to get three hits was the winner. He won nine out of ten times. It could have been ten out of ten, but he deliberately let me win so I would not get too discouraged, quit, and spoil his fun. One thing for sure, we were careful not to let Papa catch us at such play, because he would have seen it as taking up too much time and energy that could be put to better use in the fields.

As soon as our tasks were finished, we assembled at the table for breakfast. Things were timed by everyone so that we didn't have to wait for a latecomer. One of the standing rules in our household, however, was that no one tasted anything or started eating until everybody was at the table. We did not ordinarily say grace either before or after a meal. About the only time we deviated from this practice was when the preacher was visiting. In this case, we depended on him to ask the blessing.

The food was plentiful and always tasty; whenever I ate at an American's home, I was surprised how grease-free and bland their food tasted compared to ours. We could have as much of everything as we wanted, but once it was on our plate, we had to eat it all. I do not remember anybody in my family ever saying they did not like some particular dish, and we were never picky about what we ate. Papa simply would not have permitted such goings on in our household.

What leftovers there might have been were never wasted. They either went to the dogs, who hung around the back-porch steps, or were put in the hogs' slop bucket, which sat conveniently perched high on a shelf built on to the outside wall of the house. The reason it was so high was to keep the chickens and dogs out of it. The leftovers were mixed with whatever was suitable to make the slop and given to the hogs twice daily. Although I never thought about it at the time, it still amazes me to think how "tough" our hogs must have been, considering the fact that the women washed our dishes in water with a heavy dose of lye soap, and this water was then dumped in the slop bucket. It did not even keep the hogs from getting fat or even sick before they were killed.

Papa would start by first serving himself from large platters of food. These made their rounds, in order, from him to the last person. Our plates were normally heavily laden with freshly fried eggs (with lots of grease clearly visible); bacon or ham (also with lots of fat); a choice of honey, jelly, or sorghum syrup; and homemade bread and butter. Since we had no refrigeration, in the summer months the butter had the consistency of cream and also did not look too fresh after the first day. We also had plenty of fresh raw milk. If we happened to have a block of ice in the icebox, we chipped off pieces and put them in our milk glasses. But if not, we drank it while it was still warm. Other than salt and pepper, everything was grown or prepared by us on our farm and in our kitchen. Papa was the only one who had coffee, which was prepared from whole coffee beans ground in a small, hand-cranked grinder attached to the kitchen wall and boiled in a small pot. A small hand strainer was used to keep his coffee grounds out of his cup.

There was lots of conversation at the breakfast table, but we kids knew that at some point Papa would tell us about the special jobs we were to do on that day. My brother used to refer to this as time for Papa giving orders to everybody.

All of us finished eating about the same time, so no one got up or asked to be excused for any reason, and we stayed in our places until all were ready to leave the table. The men made no effort to carry their plates, leftover food, or anything else to the kitchen, since this was considered women's work. While the girls and Mama were getting things cleaned up after breakfast, we men went our separate ways to prepare for the day's work or school or some other activity.

A large variety of things were planted, and we were always jumping from one thing to another. Our major cash crop was cotton. Other things grown in the field included corn, small grains (usually sorghum cane for feed and molasses, and maize), sudan grass, oats, a few fruit trees (pear, plum, fig, and peach), sweet potatoes, Irish potatoes, watermelons, and mushmelons. A mushmelon approximated the size and shape of a football and when ripe had a yellowish-orange color and tasted like a cantaloupe. We grew enough sweet and Irish potatoes to eat the year round, storing them in a special potato house in layers of dry sand.

We Czechs had bigger gardens than the Americans, in which we planted up to as many as twenty different things. Our stock answer to an outsider's question about what we had in our garden was: "You name it, we've got it." It was highly unusual for us to buy anything to eat other than staple items from a store. This was another difference between us and the Americans, who bought a whole lot more of their food.

We saved as much seed as we could from the previous year, but we sometimes had to start with bought seed planted in carefully prepared hotbeds. The plants were carefully nurtured, watered, and then transplanted, one at a time. Each new transplant had to be watered one at a time, which required first draw-

Young Snook couples canning vegetables, about 1924. (Photograph courtesy John Fojt)

ing water from the well, carrying it in a bucket (a "pail" was something found only in our reading books), and then carefully pouring about a cupful on each individual plant without getting any water on the leaves.

Papa got the garden ready for planting each year by plowing it in neat rows. I never could figure out why he always chose our meanest and stubbornest mule (Kate) to do the garden plowing. But mainly I figured it was Papa matching his stubbornness with hers. He was determined to teach Kate who was boss, but when she felt like straying from walking a straight line, she would do just that. This resulted in a crooked furrow, something that Papa hated. He could be heard a far piece cursing the mule in a loud voice, declaring her to be a "no good _____ _____ _____. I'll teach you better than that!" This he hoped to do by yanking on her lines and beating her with a switch. But Kate seemed to have a special knack for rankling Papa, and in spite of the cursing and other threats, she never gave in. The more he fumed, the worse she would get.

I learned at an early age not to hang around too close when Papa was exasperated with Kate, because I would likely catch it, too, for no reason other than I happened to be there. But then it could have been that he had the suspicion that I was enjoying seeing Kate get the best of him. Later, after the plowing was done and Papa simmered down, when Mama thought we kids couldn't hear her, she would tell him he ought not curse like that in front of his kids. Papa would always tell Mama she was right, "but that damn mule makes me so mad I want to kill her. I'm going to break her of her meanness if it kills me." His bouts with Kate were about the only time I ever saw Papa lose at anything that really mattered to him, but she was just as contrary the day she died of old age as she was in her earlier years, in spite of the many cursings and beatings she got. When we found her dead in the pasture, I remember Papa's eyes watering up a bit and hearing him in a hoarse voice paying homage to her by admitting that she was a real strong mule, even if she was stubborn, and there was not any load she could not pull if she put her mind to it. But making her mind up to do it right was something else.

Once Papa got the garden plowed, it was up to Mama and us kids to take care of it from that point on. The plants had to be watered every afternoon after school and sometimes, during a dry spell, also in the morning before we went to school. I remember as a child thinking if God was supposed to be so good, surely he would bring us a rain so I would not have to do it all the time.

Insecticides were never used on garden crops in those days since insects were rare. About the only enemies we had were Irish potato bugs, which did not bother the sweet potatoes. As soon as they showed up, we picked them off each plant, one at a time, and put them in a tin can partly filled with kerosene from which they could not possibly ever recover. If nobody was looking, I would give the potato bugs extra punishment by lighting a match and throwing it in the can of kerosene.

The waxy black soil always could be counted on to provide an abundance of produce, and none of it was wasted. A hard-working family of seven consumed a lot of food, and we sometimes provided noon meals for our hired workers as a part of their wages. Any extra amounts were canned or given to neighbors. Also, no visitors ever went away without an ample supply of fresh vegetables. Even if they offered to pay, we would not let them, for nothing was expected in return other than a well-meant thanks. When our oversupply was so large that we could not consume it or give it away, it was given to the hogs or chickens. Sometimes I would take turnips to school and trade them for a few sheets of paper from a "Big Chief" tablet. My classmates thought it was a fair trade since the turnips tasted extra-good at noon recess, consumed raw, with no salt or anything else on them.

I always have proudly claimed that I was brought up on a fifty-acre blackland farm. But this is not exactly the truth, because we had another fifty acres of sandy pasture which was located among Americans outside our community about three miles from where we lived. It was natural, however, for us to think of our farm as being limited to the fifty acres of black, waxy soil where our house and garden and crops were located.

Papa felt that the fifty acres of black soil was as good as could be found for growing crops and, therefore, too valuable to use for pastureland and for the trees we needed for firewood. A few Czechs lived where our pasture was located, but they were biding their time until acreage would be available in the blackland section.

Very few Czechs in my community started their married lives with enough money to make a down payment for land and become farm owners. Mama and Papa were a typical example of having to make many sacrifices while they worked their way up to sharecropping and then to farm ownership. When they started their married life, they had only enough money to buy a stove, which doubled for cooking and heating for a few years until they could afford to buy a wood heater. That old stove was dear to Mama's heart, and she finally agreed to give it up long after it should have been replaced. The rest of the furniture, such as it was, was donated by Czechs in the community, or Papa and his friends made it.

Mama and Papa spent the first year of their married life farming land which a Czech owner provided rent-free in exchange for breaking a pasture and making it into land for crops. Mama's mother died the year that she and Papa married, and they moved in with my grandfather to help him and the rest of his family on their farm. After that they moved on three separate occasions, from one farm to another, as sharecroppers. They finally saved enough money to buy their own workstock and farming equipment and became one-third and one-fourth renters (paying one-third of the corn crop and one-fourth of the cotton as rent). A few years later, they bought fifty acres of pastureland outside the Snook community while continuing to farm rented land within the community's boundaries. Finally in 1928 — after twenty-three years of being renters — they made a down payment on the fifty-acre place which we always referred to as our farm. The other fifty acres of sandy land, to us, was just pastureland that we happened to own.

Mama and Papa had the misfortune of trying to pay off our farm during a difficult period of very low cotton prices. When they made the first down payment, cotton was bringing twenty-eight to thirty cents per pound but dropped to between four and eight cents per pound during the next seven years.

Among the many events that stand out clearly in my mind is Mama and Papa sharing their plight with their children. We owed five thousand dollars we borrowed from the SPJST to buy our fifty-acre farm. For three years in a row, the SPJST let us get by without paying anything on the principal as long as we paid the interest. After paying this amount and the stores, the blacksmith shop, and the garage for the things we charged in Snook, we had very little money left. So only those of us that had holes in the soles of our shoes got a new pair. The rest had to wait until better times.

Mama and Papa finally paid off their debt on the fifty acres after all of their children left home. Cotton prices were good during World War II, and they paid off the SPJST in 1945. So seventeen years after borrowing the money and forty years after they first started farming, they finally were full-fledged owners of their fifty-acre blackland farm.

Although I never was so bold as to directly question Papa's wisdom in the matter, I could not fully appreciate why he used all of the blackland where we lived for crops, a garden, and a small hay meadow, and none of it for pasture. This probably was because I spent so many hours shuttling cows and mules back and forth between the two places and checking on our hogs and turkeys. I made an average of about seventy round trips — one hour each way — between the pasture and our farm in a calendar year. The degree of frequency depended on the different times of the year and how often and how much it rained. Papa figured that the more he could keep our animals in the pasture, the less feedstuff we had to grow on the blackland for their use, and the more land could be used for cotton and corn crops and food for our family.

When some of the mules were needed on our farm, I walked to the pasture late on Sunday afternoons and brought them home. Catching the mules usually was not too big a job, because they knew they would get some corn that had been put in the feedlot. Mules are dumb creatures in some ways, but smart in others. Some might consider them to be dumb since they could be tricked into coming inside the lot for a few ears of corn. But I found out that they were also smart. If I did not give them some corn, the next time they would not come on their own, and I had to go out into the pasture and force them to go into the lot. If there was to be any trouble getting all eight mules in the pen, there never was any doubt which one would be the problem — Kate. I could count on her to test my ingenuity to figure out new ways to trick her into it and to get the gate shut before she decided she wanted back out again.

Once the mules were in the pen, I would put a bridle on my favorite — Mary — so I could ride her bareback on the way home, while the others (except Kate) were herded along sort of like cattle. But Kate had to be bridled and led on a rope, because she had a knack for straying in some unexpected direction which sometimes caused the other mules to follow her lead. Most of the time there was no problem taking the mules from the pasture to the farm except when an infrequent car came along or a snake or varmint crossed the road and spooked them. Sometimes Kate decided to be stubborn and determined not to cross one of the larger bridges. But on the whole, these were good learning experiences and taught me to deal with adversity.

In some ways our mules were like people. Some would lead, while others would follow. Some would balk and shirk, but others would overdo. One or two would dominate the rest, driving them away from the feed, water tank, or salt block. Some would kick and nip, but others had such friendly dispositions that even a small child could walk around or under them with the greatest of ease. It did not take long to find out what type a new mule would be, and we quickly learned how to behave around her.

Being balky meant just stopping in her tracks and refusing to pull, turn, or do anything else. Kate epitomized the balky, stubborn type, while Emma and Mary were the most gentle and cooperative. Because they were different, they gained or lost in some ways. When I fed the mules, my partiality became obvious. If there were a few extra ears of corn, they invariably ended up in the feedboxes in Mary's and Emma's stalls rather than Kate's. If I fed them freshly cut cane, green oat stalks, or fodder, Kate would get less than her share. But then, when it came time to pick out a mule to do something in which only one was needed, then Emma or Mary drew the assignment. I always thought Kate somehow knew this in her own way and got special pleasure out of getting the last laugh on me after all.

One time Papa decided to see if the mules would follow behind our car if we led Mary on a rope. Of course, that meant also putting a rope around Kate's neck and leading her, too. With Papa driving and me holding the two ropes, all went well until about halfway home, when Kate suddenly decided not to cooperate, stopping dead still in her tracks. Papa could not stop quickly. Instead of turning loose of the rope, I gripped it even tighter. Kate gave me a good case of rope-burned hands. She got a good cursing and bridle yanking from Papa, and I got a few days off from heavy work. But that's the last time we tried to bring the mules home in this fashion when Kate was among them.

As soon as we were through with the mules on Friday afternoons, or when it rained a lot, I took them back to the pasture pretty much in the same way they were brought home. But they always had more pep and acted more frisky when we were headed for the pasture than when we were coming in a homeward direction. It was as if they knew that they would have some time off from work chores and being yelled at by Papa. Even Kate behaved herself better when headed for the pasture than in the opposite direction. And I was happier, too, knowing there would be less hard work for a day or two.

We Czechs had mules for our workstock and then maybe a horse, but only if we had some special reason to have one. The Americans, on the other hand, had horses first and then maybe a mule or two. This difference probably was because we were dirt farmers and needed the type of workstock that could pull heavy loads and for which mules were best suited. The Americans, who had more cattle and less farmland, found horses to be more suitable for their purposes.

We normally kept anywhere between six and eight mules and had only one horse, just for a very short time. Papa really did not want to own a horse, but he got it from an American who had borrowed ten dollars and gave it to us to pay off his debt. Papa said several times that he really did not want the horse, because any animal that could not earn his keep was not worth having. If we needed something to ride, then a good mule did double duty. He traded the horse to another American as soon as he got his first chance to do so.

The first Czechs who came to Texas used oxen and horses for their workstock but found out that the horses were a mistake. Although very few who emigrated to the United States had owned any kind of animals as a source of work power, they were accustomed to seeing horses on farms in the Old Country. But there was one big difference. Those in Europe were the large, draft-type horses that were good for pulling heavy loads. Not realizing that there were basic differences between the European-type draft horses and the ones they first bought in the United States, they found out that those here were more skittish, harder to handle, and more prone to get sick and did not have the toughness and pulling power they wanted. So they switched to the more docile, tougher, and stronger mule. As a result, the Czechs in my community looked upon horses with some disdain as more or less useless animals that they could do without. On the other hand, they placed great stock in their mules.

Papa was proudest of two pairs of mules we owned, his first choice being Emma and Mary, who were an off-white color, and his second choice, Tobe and Mabel, a grayish, smaller pair. Everyone in our community recognized Emma and Mary on sight and had some appreciation for how fine a pair they made. Papa's eyes would light up when somebody would say they wished they had a pair of mules like Emma and Mary. He never failed to show them off when he had the chance to do so. But he was not too proud to be seen with Kate and her partner, Jack. Consequently Shine, our black hired hand, always drew Kate and Jack whenever we had to have all of our mules where other people saw them. In fact, Papa was so proud of Emma and Mary that they were outfitted with the best of harnesses when there was not enough money to have first-class harnesses for all of the mules.

Although mules were tough when compared to horses and cattle, occasionally they would turn up sick. Since we did not have a veterinarian in our community or nearby, Papa did his own diagnoses of what was wrong. Two particular situations come to mind.

If a mule looked sickly and had a habit of putting her head to one side, Papa's diagnosis was that she had the "bots." I never knew what this term was supposed to mean medically, but it was a condition where a mule had worms in its stomach. Papa always kept a supply of medicine on hand to treat this condition. It was in the form of a thick, black syrupy substance supposedly similar to screwworm medicine. This was slightly diluted with a mixture of water and kerosene and poured into a Nehi soda-water bottle. While a couple of strong men forced the sick animal to hold its head up. Papa poked the bottle down its throat and forced it to drink the nasty concoction. After a short waiting period, the mule would defecate. The worms, which looked sort of like tapeworms, would be clearly visible, and Papa would pronounce the whole operation a success. By the next day, the mule was chipper and ready to go.

If a mule became unusually lethargic, lay down, and did not want to get up, then Papa's diagnosis was the colic. In this case, a concoction of regular cooking soda mixed in water ended up in the same Nehi bottle, and the mule was forced to swallow it. Shortly afterward, a good healthy belch or a loud passage of gas, and possibly both, would be forthcoming. Papa would then pronounce the mule to be O.K. Papa must have been a good diagnostician, because I do not remember a mule of ours ever dying of anything other than old age.

Since we Czechs were self-sufficient farmers, a variety of livestock and poultry was a part of our operations. Typically, we had between ten and fifteen head of cattle. Usually only one or two cows we were milking and their suckling calves were kept at home. The rest stayed on a year-round basis in our pasture.

Papa was partial to red bald-faced cattle, which he thought produced better beef, so we never had any of the better types of milk producers such as Jerseys or Guernseys.

I did not mind milking cows any more than any other farm chore, but sometimes it became odious. This was when it rained a lot in the winter months and the cow lot got real mucky. Since we had no gutters to drain the water away from the cow shed and the lot was poorly drained, the mixture of cow manure, urine, water, and mud would get real soft. My rubber boots would sink as much as six inches deep in the muck. But that was not the most unpleasant part. The worst was when the end of the cow's tail got soaked and dirty from muck on a real cold day and she managed to score a direct hit with her tail across my face while I was milking. As a result of these conditions, little specks of muck found their way into my milk bucket. But this did not particularly bother anybody, because most of the specks were caught by the strainer before we actually drank the milk. And none of us ever suffered any consequences of drinking raw milk even if it had a few specks. In fact, we thrived on it. One of the ways we enjoyed fresh milk was by seasoning it with sugar, vanilla, and nutmeg and pouring it over fresh snow (on the rare occasions when it snowed). Not only did it make a good substitute for ice cream, but also the nutmeg made the specks less noticeable.

One lesson I learned about milking was to get it done fast, because a cow might not want to stand still after the little amount of feed she got (usually cottonseed hulls or corn shucks) was eaten, and that could create a problem. I did not dare just give up milking if this happened, because my sisters always took note of any shortages when they strained the milk for either breakfast or supper, and Papa would find out about it for sure.

As with everything else we produced, none of the milk was ever wasted. What we did not drink was left to sit and form cream on the top and the rest to sour and turn into clabber. Cream skimmed off the top had many uses. It was eaten with jelly or molasses and fresh homemade bread, used in mashed potatoes or in cooking, or made into butter. What was left over was traded to a local store even if it was on the verge of becoming rancid, along with our extra eggs. Some of the clabber was dumped in an empty cloth sugar sack which hung from a nail over a bucket on the back porch. When all of the liquid was drained, Mama made it into a real tasty kolache filling by seasoning it with sugar, butter, and fresh eggs. The drained-off liquid either became a part of the hog slop or was dumped in the chicken troughs.

Sometimes I took the extra cream and eggs to the store to be traded in or credited on whatever was bought. After the storekeeper weighed the cream, he sometimes asked me to dump it in a big milk can along with the rest he bought from other farmers. The cream smelled pretty strong sometimes, especially when it was on its third or fourth day of a hot summer. Ours usually smelled pretty mild compared with the cream in the container it was dumped in. One time I asked the storekeeper how far gone the cream had to be for him to turn it down. His reply was that as long as it did not have maggots in it, he would buy it. I often wondered what the buyers of the cream did with it after they picked it up from the storekeeper but never was brave enough to ask. After telling my sisters about the rancid cream, they would not eat any store-bought cheese or ice cream for about a month after that. But it did not bother my brothers or me one bit.

The storekeeper bought all of the Snook farmers' extra eggs regardless of their freshness up until the early 1930s. But then he got a Delco system installed and had a light bulb mounted in a box which had a round hole in it slightly smaller than the size of an egg. If he could see the shadow of the yolk, then he pronounced it to be fertile and would not buy it. We took the eggs home he would not buy and used them just as we would any other egg and never suffered any consequences.

Ptacek's general merchandise store in Snook in the 1920s. (Photograph courtesy Ed J. Ptacek) BELOW: *Fojt's general merchandise store in the Snook business section, about 1925. Note the public outhouse, right rear of store.* (Photograph courtesy John Fojt)

One of the advantages of growing up around farm animals was that I did not have to be told about the birds and the bees, because we kids got to see such activities at a very early age. I saw my first baby pigs being born when I was about age five, and as a youngster I assisted Papa many times in the birthing of a calf. At about age eight, I took a mare we owned for a short time to have her bred to a donkey and then saw her give birth to a baby mule as a result of this mating. Papa sent me to the pasture occasionally to check on a cow to see if she had given birth to a calf. Also, I watched hogs and young bull calves being castrated. And we even got to eat the resultant fried mountain oysters, which we were taught to believe were a delicacy.

In some ways, cattle were more trouble than mules. They tended to get sick more often, attract more flies, get bloated from eating too much clover, and break down more fences and were more likely to have worms.

Screwworms got started in open lesions, usually caused by a cow hooking another with her horns or by cutting herself on a barbed-wire fence. (It was never pronounced "barbed wire" in Snook, but always "bob wire".) The worms multiplied rapidly and ate away at the flesh, which was clearly visible to the naked eye. Cattle had to be checked often, particularly in the summertime, to make sure they did not have worms. When they did, we scooped them out with a stick or swab and drenched the lesion with a smelly worm medicine. The whole thing was then coated with axle grease to prevent flies from causing another infestation in the same lesion, but that did not guarantee that they would not come back.

Each spring, our pasture had a lot of luscious clover. As our cows gorged themselves on it, the mixture of liquids and fresh grass formed large quantities of a gaseous substance in their rumen. This would cause them to swell up and have difficulty breathing. This was called the "bloat." Although we never lost a cow on account of the bloat, there were stories of those who did. Two remedies were tried. One was to pry the cow's mouth open and tie a stick in it, running crosswise, and then make her run for a distance. If this worked, the foul-smelling gaseous material would come out from both ends, and this took care of it. If this did not work, we stuck a narrow pointed butcher knife a certain depth in an indented section between the last rib and the hipbone. The knife punctured the rumen, and the gaseous condition would be relieved in this way. Sometimes one could hear the released gas, which sounded similar to letting air out of a tire. The punctured spot would heal itself in due time with no apparent harm done to the cow.

In 1925, we had a severe drought which limited the amount of grass, hay, fodder, or anything else we produced as feed. Our cattle lost a lot of weight and were more susceptible to problems in giving birth to calves. Sometimes a cow got so weak she could not stand up after having a calf. We had to lift her onto a homemade sled, haul her to the barn, and take special care of her while helping her to regain her strength. Since she could not stand up, we had to milk her and then trick her calf into drinking the milk by sticking our fingers in the milk to act as substitute teats.

When a calf was born dead, or if it did not suck enough milk after it had been born, the mother cow would get what we called milk fever. This condition was relieved by more frequent milking. I do not remember any cow of ours dying from milk fever but heard stories about some of the Americans losing cows that way.

We had a dreadful fear of the blackleg in both cattle and workstock. Sometimes someone's animal died, and word would be spread that it was the blackleg. But this rumor probably was not correct. Anyway, none of our animals ever got the blackleg.

Of course, other farm animals became sick or developed diseases just like humans. Our hogs and chickens got worms, just as our mules did, but the treatment was different. As soon as the worms became visible in the hogs' feces, Papa dumped ashes in their slop. After a day or two, the hogs' feces became clear, and it was free of worms. Occasionally, hogs developed something similar to mange in dogs. Our treatment for it was a good rubbing over the entire body of the hog with burned automobile lube oil. This was dirty, thick oil that had been drained from a crankcase.

Sometimes our chickens developed what Papa diagnosed as cholera when their droppings were runny and they had an excessive amount of molting. It was treated by skimming bark from a blackjack tree, boiling it in water, and substituting this concoction in their water troughs for their regular water.

A number of things stand out in my mind very vividly in handling our cattle. One was that sometime in the late 1920s, our entire county had an infestation of ticks which caused a disease called Texas tick fever. All cattle were quarantined and had to be dipped in a public dipping vat several times. My sister and I had to drive our cattle on foot about two and a half miles each way to have them dipped. Since the vat was located in the general area of our pasture, most of the others using it were Americans who herded their cattle on horses. We just knew that the Americans made fun of us behind our backs because Papa sent his children on foot to do a job they were having grown men on horses do.

The year 1925 was exceptionally dry. Our stock tank and creeks went dry, and the water in our well was too salty to use for either man or beast. For at least a couple of weeks that summer before it finally rained, my sister and I had to drive our cattle on foot every day about three miles each way to an unfenced creek fed by a spring, so that they could get their fill of water.

Livestock prices varied a great deal when I was a youngster. Although we really did not have cattle for the money we could make from their sale, we sold an occasional steer, cow, or calf. Every penny they brought was welcome. In the early 1920s, they brought a good price. But in the latter 1920s and early 1930s, cattle prices hit rock bottom.

One time in the early 1930s, Papa tried to sell a cow and a calf, both in good condition, for $7.50, but had no takers.

Since there was little or no grass in the wintertime, the cattle had to be fed things grown on our farm just to keep them alive. When they got so low in price, the federal government sponsored a program to pay a farmer the going price for a cow and destroy it. Papa wrestled with his conscience over the question of whether or not to participate in the program. While he felt it was not right for the government to kill cattle, he needed what little money they would bring, and it would also save on the amount of feed we had to produce on our farm. After much deliberation, he had four head killed by the government, but it bothered him a great deal. If anyone ever brought up the subject, he did not want to talk about it.

We used our pasture not only for mules and cattle, but also for our hogs and turkeys during certain times of the year.

Around mid-October, post-oak and live-oak acorns began to fall on the ground and were an important source of food for our hogs. Instead of feeding them corn and slop at home, we would take a sow and her litter (of five to eight pigs) to the pasture after they had been weaned. There they were allowed to roam freely. None of the pastures adjoining ours had hog fences, so the pigs often got in someone else's pasture, and likewise theirs could feed in ours. We cut an identifying notch, or notches, in each pig's ear and that became our special mark of recognition.

When the pigs were supposed to be in our pasture or somewhere else nearby, someone had to check on them every few days. Papa taught me how to call our hogs in a special way, since they seldom were visible in the thick yaupon underbrush and trees. A good hog caller and a few ears of corn as bait brought the pigs running. Once they were checked on, they were then left alone to roam until the next time. If one or two got mixed in with ours, we let their owners know where they could be found, and they returned the favor if any of ours wandered off and joined theirs. We were not afraid of having our pigs stolen or harmed if they strayed off on someone else's property, and we never lost a hog. They were fattened up on acorns, berries, grass, and weeds and were in good shape to be killed the next time a good norther came through. If they were not fat enough, we took them back to our farm and fattened them before the next hog-killing time.

Turkeys, like mules or cattle, came in different colors and sizes. Although some refer to them as being dumb, they also can be smart. Our turkeys mixed with the rest of the poultry at feeding time but got off in their own group at other times. They found unusual places to roost separately and also to lay their eggs.

Turkeys loved grasshoppers. Sometimes their craws became so filled with undigested grasshoppers they became top heavy, staggered, and had a dazed look. When this happened, their craws were slit open with a sharp knife, the grasshoppers were removed (some still alive and kicking), and their craws were sewed back up with a needle and thread. As soon as we had them sewed up and turned loose, they acted as if nothing had happened and caught and swallowed the first grasshopper that came their way. Their craws always healed without any difficulty, and the turkeys were no worse off from their encounters with knife, needle, and thread.

We sometimes took our turkeys to the pasture and left them there for a month or two, checking on them every few days. Papa taught me how to sound like a gobbler, which brought them running because they knew they would get some corn.

Our turkeys laid more eggs in the pasture than when we kept them on our farm. We used them for hatching and sold the excess to local farmers. They were very skillful at picking out places to lay their eggs which were hard to find. Once the eggs had been located and in any way disturbed, the turkeys abandoned that location and found another place to lay their eggs.

Occasionally a skunk or snake found a nest and ate the eggs. One summer, we were sure something was getting some of the turkey eggs. Papa, figuring that it was a snake, skillfully emptied the contents from their shells and filled them with a poisonous material, hoping to poison the culprit. The next day, my sisters' favorite dog, Snowball, was missing. After an extended search, we found him dead. It has been Snowball who had been eating the eggs. Although Mama sympathized with my sisters, who cried over losing their precious pet, Papa made it known that any dog that ate turkey eggs should have been dead a whole lot sooner.

Although our pasture was fairly small, it was a source of sustenance in other ways than just the grass, acorns, and grasshoppers. The stock tank normally had fish and crawfish, and we spent many hours contentedly trying our luck, but seldom catching enough for a meal. It also had big bullfrogs, which provided tasty frog legs, fried in cornmeal, for an occasional breakfast.

My middle brother set out traps for wild animals. Whenever he caught something, the hides were sold for a small amount of money. We also used the tank for swimming since there was not a swimming pool anywhere in our entire county. We hunted doves and occasionally killed a rabbit or squirrel, all of which were cooked and eaten.

Among the things I enjoyed most about our pasture were picking pecans, dewberries, wild plums, and mustang grapes. Pecans were my extra source of money in the winter months. Often on Saturday mornings, I walked to the pasture with a sandwich of sausage and homemade bread and picked pecans. When I felt especially adventurous, I slipped over into one of the neighboring pastures and picked theirs also, even though I knew I was not supposed to. While I left some of the pecans at home for family use, I took most of them to the store, where I got one, and sometimes, two cents per pound. While this seems a small amount compared to today's prices, a nickel in those days bought a large sack of candy and licorice big enough for me to share with my brothers and sisters and still have quite a bit left over for my own enjoyment. Jelly beans and sugar-coated peanuts were our favorites.

We picked wild plums and dewberries, which grew profusely in our pasture, and made jellies and jams for the family members to enjoy. My sisters were afraid that the dewberry vines, overgrown with weeds and bushes, harbored snakes and always were on the lookout for them. I might have been a little skeptical, too, but the boy in me would never permit me to admit it. Invariably when we picked dewberries, some horror story about snakes would come up. My sisters sincerely believed an often-repeated tale about an expectant mother becoming frightened upon seeing a snake while picking berries, thus causing her child to have birthmarks, and even in some cases to be epileptic. The dewberries mostly ended up in jelly, but we also ate them fresh with sugar and with fresh milk. But our favorite was fresh dewberry cobbler, eaten when it was still warm.

Picking wild mustang grapes was the men's job since they grew on vines high in trees, and we had to use ladders to get to them. They were picked at two different times. The first was when they were still green, these being made into a tart-tasting jelly and green-grape pie. When they were fully ripened, Papa used them for making wine.

We kept beehives in our pasture, in addition to those at our homeplace. We learned not to agitate them, because their sting could be deadly. The real excitement took place when they swarmed and found a resting place, usually on a tree branch. Papa then put on a special homemade mask of heavy cotton-sacking material sewed around screen wire through which he could see, heavy leather gloves, and heavy clothing, making sure that all parts of his body were fully covered. Armed with a smoke blower, he was good at capturing the bees. Even so, he got an occasional sting, causing him to utter a few curse words and crush the guilty bee, even though it would have died anyway when it lost its stinger. His explanation for the strong language was that it was a natural reaction and that a bee sting would make even a preacher curse.

The Americans didn't make nearly as much use of their

grapes, berries, wild plums, and pecans as we Czechs did. Also, none of them had bees. Both parents and children had more free time to ride horses and do other kinds of things. Sometimes they made fun of us Czechs for working so hard. But we did not mind their remarks too much. After all, we were brought up to believe that the things we were doing benefited our families as a whole, and that was reason enough for us to be proud of being different.

In some ways, making hay was a distasteful job since it was dusty, hard work and took place in the hottest part of the year. But the good thing about it was that it lasted for only a few days.

Every farm in our community had at least a small hay meadow. Ours was about five acres in size. The black, waxy soil grew a mixture of prairie grasses, sometimes knee-deep, and it made good-quality prairie hay. Most of the time we even got two good cuttings in one year. All of it was made into bales, because Czechs thought that hay put up in stacks was not as good a quality as when it was baled. The sandy land occupied by the Americans could not grow good prairie hay, so they broadcast cane and put it up in stacks.

Although the cost of equipment for baling hay was only a proverbial drop in the bucket compared with today's prices, it was too expensive for us to own all of it. Each farmer had only one or two pieces, so we pooled our labor and equipment and put our hay up together as a team effort, with each farmer keeping the bales produced from his own meadow.

Since we owned the mowing machine, we cut our meadow first. As soon as we finished, one of our Czech neighbors got it and mowed his. Then the third farmer did the same.

While the freshly cut grass was drying in the hot sun and turning a light-tan color, the baling equipment was being readied for action. From the time the first blade of grass was mowed, everybody hoped that a rain or local late-afternoon thundershower did not develop. The one thing they did not want was

Snook Czech farmers baling hay, about 1932. (Photograph courtesy Adolf Vajdak)

for the hay to be rained on before it was safely put away in the barn.

While the third farmer's mowing was being done, all of the equipment for baling was set in place in our meadow. But we had to wait until the morning dew had disappeared before we started—sometimes even as late as nine o'clock. This seemed awkward since everything else we did normally would have started a full three, or even three and a half, hours earlier. While the men traded jobs, depending on whose hay we were baling, Shine was the only permanent fixture. He fed the baler, no matter whose hay was being worked.

I had a hand at every job that goes with baling hay except Shine's spot. At about age six, I followed a pair of mules around and around in a continuous circle as they provided the power to operate the hay baler. Later, I graduated to punching wires through the wooden blocks that separated each bale of hay;

then tying the wires; operating the windrow rake and the bull rake; and pitching the hay up to a position where Shine needed it to feed the press.

Shine, the only black among as many as twelve to twenty Czechs, was always in his glory when he was feeding the baler. It was hard work, and it did not take long for the sweat to start pouring off every part of his body. But he got great pleasure out of being able to shout, "More hay!" at the white men who were throwing it to where he needed it for the next thrust downward into the baler. There was not a farmer in the entire community that did not hear about how good Shine was at feeding the baler, and he was very proud of his well-earned reputation. He got no extra pay for doing this extra-hard work but was pleased with the opportunity each year to prove again that he was the best there was at it.

Everybody working around the hay baler had to be alert at what they were doing, as it was a matter of teamwork at its best. As the compressed hay moved forward through the baler, a wooden block was inserted by Shine following each seventh forkful of hay. The block had an upper and lower slot on both sides through which two wires (one near the top, one near the bottom) were punched. The person on the other side tied the two ends together in a loose, but firm, fashion. With each circle made by the mules and each stroke by the baler, the hay moved forward one block at a time until the bale popped out. As it did so, the wires which had been loosely tied became taut when the bale expanded after having been so tightly compressed.

About the only time I disrupted the hay-baling operation in any way was when I performed the job of wire puncher. This was a very slow-moving, boring, and monotonous job for a boy ten or eleven years of age. My mind wandered to more pleasant matters, and occasionally I put one of the wires on the wrong side of the block, thus attaching the block to the bale. This meant that the entire bale had to be cut loose with wire cutters and fed through all over again. I hoped Papa wouldn't be around to remind me to keep my mind on what I was doing when it happened. Some of the workers showed a little disgust at having to run the hay through a second time and ruining two strands of baling wire. But good-natured Shine just laughed and teased me about getting my mind off some pretty girl and putting it back on punching wires. As the bales spewed forth out of the baler, they were put on a wagon, hauled off, and stacked in the barn by other workers.

When we got through baling our hay, the operation was moved to the second farmer's meadow, and the whole process started all over again. In turn, after that was finished, we moved to the third farmer's meadow. The entire operation was a co-operative effort that ran smoothly without any disagreements. If one farmer had three sons available to help while another had only two, this didn't make any difference. Likewise, if one had a four-acre meadow and another five acres, this, too, made no difference. No money ever changed hands among the three farmers, and if one family made a larger contribution toward getting everybody's hay hauled than another, then that's just the way it was. We never kept track of these differences, because we knew each family did all they could to make the whole thing a success, and we were all happy to have our hay safely in the barn with a minimum of cost.

The three Czech families spent a lot of time together when we made hay. The women cooked big dinners for everybody and alternated houses where we ate dinner each day. After all the haying was done, each family made a freezer of different-flavored ice cream, and we all got together to celebrate the occasion. Unlike us, the Americans did not pool their resources and cooperate with each other in these kinds of endeavors. Whatever hay baling they did was on an individual family basis. If their neighbors helped, they were paid money for it. Or if they did not have all the equipment, they rented it from Papa or someone else on a cash basis.

3.

Hard Work in the Fields

Our garden had something growing in it the year round, a few vegetables being planted more than one time every year. But the field crops were produced only once a year. Of these, cotton got by far the most attention. It was our only cash crop, and our economic success or failure was largely determined by how much we produced and the price we got for it. We also spent more hours and worked harder in the cotton fields than all of the rest of the crops put together. For the most part, it was boring, and after a few days in the cotton field it became a test of endurance where strong backs, legs, arms, and a lot of patience were required. Like the rest of my young cohorts, I did not know much about occupational opportunities, but I knew that spending the rest of my life in a cotton patch was the last thing I wanted to do.

Breaking the land, or busting it, as it was called by us Czechs, was the last thing we did after harvesting a crop. But it also was the first thing to get it ready for the next crop season. This was no job for a youngster or woman, because it took a strong person skilled at handling two teams of mules and guiding the middlebuster at the same time. It was about the only job I never did, because Papa thought I was too young.

Just harnessing up four mules abreast in pairs of two and getting them properly hitched to the middlebuster was no small assignment. Needless to say, Kate never was selected, because the mules had to work well together. Even then, Papa would lose his temper and could be heard cursing a mule that went too fast or lagged behind the others. But when Papa or Shine, our hired hand, had a fistful of lines in hand and shouted "Get up," it was a beautiful sight to see. As the middlebuster turned over the rich black soil, it glistened as the sun hit it at the right angle. It took a skillful driver to make sure that every furrow was straight. Papa used to say it looked too much like an American's field if a furrow was crooked, and it would not ever do for us Czechs. If all of this was not demanding enough on Papa or Shine, there was the additional task of turning the mules at the end of each row. There was a real art to turning just right so the ends of the rows were straight, all of the old stalks were covered, and the inside mule on a turn did not get outside her traces.

Once the middlebusting was done, the land was considered to be laid by until the next year's cotton crop was planted. While the term "laid by" implied that nothing was to be done in the field, this was not the case. Cockleburs and other weeds sprouted up through the soil. When they grew a few inches in height, we had to chop them down because Papa could not stand to see weeds growing in our field. The Americans who lived nearby let their weeds grow, knowing that they did not do any harm either to the soil or to next year's crop, but our land naturally had to be cleaner than theirs.

In between the time the land was laid by and planting next year's crops, there were many things other than chopping weeds to be done. We fixed fences, built or repaired storage sheds and barns, got all of the plows in shape and plowshares sharpened, replaced old double- or singletrees and outworn harness parts, repaired wagon beds, and made wood for our stoves. Papa had a forge and blower at home, so we did a lot of our own repair work instead of having to pay for it.

Being the youngest, I did not get to work in off-season tasks as much as my brothers. Instead, I was the errand boy. When they were sawing boards, hammering nails, sharpening tools, and learning these kinds of practical skills, I held the boards in place while they nailed, turned the large round whet-

A Snook lad poses with four mules abreast hitched to a middlebuster plow, about 1934. (Photograph courtesy Ella Orsak)

stone (or blower in the blacksmith shop) by hand while they sharpened tools, and held the axle-grease bucket while they applied the grease. I also was sent to the store to get the things they needed for a particular job while they did the actual work.

Building up a supply of wood when the land was laid by had to be done every year. My brothers, Papa, Shine, and I would head for our pasture early in the morning on a wagon, with all of the needed equipment, to work for the next few days on trees Papa had carefully preselected. He favored post oaks which did not have any knots and were the right diameter for splitting. They also were located where they could be reached without too much difficulty, and the split wood could be stacked to season for a while before it was hauled to the house. I appreciated Papa's skill at picking the right trees, because there were definite differences in the amount of heat they would produce. Since this was our only source, it was important that it be good wood for all purposes.

Once we got to the trees Papa had picked out, we went to work. Two of us operated a crosscut saw, one on each end, down on our knees to cut the tree as low to the ground as possible. This was because Papa could not stand any wasted wood, and he thought high stumps were unsightly in a pasture. The first few strokes were sort of awkward while the two of us got used to each other, but once adjusted, it went smoothly and gave us a good feeling to work well together. Papa always was on hand to direct us about the side of the tree where we were to start our sawing and the proper angle of the cut so it would fall in the spot just where he wanted it.

Once the tree hit the ground, the branches too small for our purposes were cut off and stacked in a pile to be burned after they had dried. Papa decided the thickness for branches that would be either discarded or made into firewood. Next, we used the crosscut saw to cut the newly fallen tree in blocks about eighteen inches in length so they would fit in both our cookstove and our heater. The hardest job of all was splitting the green wooden blocks into individual sticks of the desired thickness. The cookstove wood was thinner, as a general rule, than the heater wood.

I was not as good at splitting wood as Papa, Shine, or my brothers. Consequently, I ended up with the other jobs — stacking the unwanted branches and separating the wood they had split and putting it in different-sized piles. The discarded branches were burned very carefully at a later date so as not to cause a fire that might damage the remaining trees or the grass.

Papa always got itchy around mid-February about planting our field crops. He had a reputation to uphold of being the first, or among the very first, to plant. Other farmers followed his lead, so if he made the mistake of planting either too early or too late, he had more at stake than just how good his own crop would turn out. He read farm magazines and studied long-range weather forecasts, consulted the *Farmer's Almanac* and *Hospodář, (Husbandman)*, and observed local signs ranging from the budding of redbuds and other trees to the actions of animals and insects. But he normally was ready to go shortly after mid-February. Corn and the feed crops normally were planted as much as a full month before cotton, which did better in warmer weather.

The methods of selecting corn and cotton seed to plant changed quite a bit during my boyhood years. In my earlier years, we grew our own seed and selected it during the regular picking seasons.

When we pulled our corn, usually in October or November, Papa had each of us take a towsack, tie a loop of binder twine to the open top, and slip the sack on our shoulder so that the open end hung about waist-high. He showed us how to look for the best-looking ears (usually the largest which pushed out through the end of the dry shucks). As we found the best ears, we dropped them in the sack while the rest of the corn was thrown directly in the wagon. As the sack load became heavier and the twine cut deeper and deeper into our shoulders, we dumped the load in one corner of the wagon. When the wagon was unloaded in the barn, the special ears we had selected were kept separately in sacks. Shortly before planting time, the seed corn was graded. That meant, after shelling, it was spread out on wire mesh of a particular size. The kernels that fell through ended up as chicken or hog feed. Those that passed the test were used for planting.

In either the late 1920s or early 1930s, Papa read about a new yellow-dent hybrid corn that had been developed which was touted as outproducing the old, regular type of corn. After discussing it with the county agricultural agent, he secretly ordered some of the seed. The reason for his secretiveness was that he was regarded as a leader in the community and did not want to do anything that might appear to have been foolish if it did not work. As it turned out, it was not much of a secret.

A Snook farmer and his niece standing beside a wagon on their way to the field to pull corn, about 1936. (Photograph courtesy Ella Orsak)

The rural mail carrier was a friendly and talkative sort of fellow. When he stopped at the Snook post office, somebody saw the sack in his car and asked him about it. He spilled the beans, saying that he thought it was some kind of seed corn "Mr. John" had ordered. By the time it was delivered by the mail carrier to our box, probably about an hour later, most of the Snook farmers already knew that Papa was going to try some kind of newfangled corn seed. No one mentioned it, but we noticed that all of a sudden after the corn was planted that year, more than the usual number of people passed by on the road next to our cornfield. Later, we figured out that apparently they were looking at the cornfield to see if they could tell the difference in the old and new type of corn Papa had planted.

Luckily for Papa, the bought seed outproduced everything else in the community. The next season, over half of the farmers switched to the new kind of seed he had planted. I was glad it turned out that way. Not only had Papa proved again he was a leader among the Czechs, but also the Americans had to admit he had beaten them again productionwise, by a wide margin. But the main reason I was glad was that it put an end to our having to go through the seed-selecting process since we bought our seed from that point on. A part of the reason we began buying our seed may also have been that this was about the time when weevils first began to attack our corn after it had been stored in the barn for a few months. We could not find a way to stop them from it. So we would have been hard put to have actually kept any seed corn until it was time to plant without it being full of weevils. This would have necessitated picking out each undamaged kernel by hand, and the weevils seemed to be smart enough to prefer the largest kernels, which would also have made the best seed corn.

The procedure for selecting cotton seed for planting in the 1920s was similar to, yet a little different from, that used in selecting seed corn. When we picked our cotton in July, all of our family members, including Mama and my sisters, went to a different part of the field from our field hands. Papa instructed us to pick only the largest and fluffiest open bolls, while the hired hands were picking all of the open cotton on each stalk. Picking only selected bolls not only was more time-consuming but also was much more tiring. Had we been picking all of the open cotton, we would have been wearing homemade knee-pads and literally crawling on our knees from one plant to another. But picking bolls selectively for seed meant a lot of alternating between an upright and stooping position, and our backs got awfully tired after being at it from sunup to sundown.

After weighing each sack of cotton, which usually was between thirty and thirty-five pounds, we had to carry our bulky loads on our shoulders more than one hundred yards to the barn. But the field hands got to empty their sacks directly into the wagon in the cotton field. Since all of us had our own sacks, Mama and my sisters had to carry their own. But they never complained about how heavy they were. The sacks were emp-

A Czech farmwife picking cotton, about 1933. She is crawling on her knees to avoid stooping all day long. (Photograph courtesy Reynalda Janac)

tied in one of the rooms in the barn that had been cleaned out for that purpose. After emptying our sacks, we usually stopped at the house to get a drink of water and sometimes a slice of homemade bread and a mixture of cream and jelly, if it was around 10:00 in the morning or 3:00 in the afternoon. Then back to the field we went to repeat the routine.

It normally took the seven of us at least two days, and sometimes longer, to pick the fifteen hundred pounds normally required for a bale. The Snook gin was not equipped to handle anything less than a bale, which normally ended up weighing around five hundred pounds of lint cotton. This yielded us about one thousand pounds of cotton seed for next year's planting. It was put in gunnysacks and remained in the barn until the following March when it would be used. Luckily, there were no insects or weevils to bother the cotton seed. Since we usually did not need over six hundred to seven hundred pounds of seed cotton for our own use and Papa had a reputation for getting high cotton yields, someone would buy the extra seed from us. Our American neighbors did not go to all of the trouble to select their own seed since they knew that Papa would sell them what he had left over. I do not suppose he thought it was unfair, but he charged the Americans a few more cents per pound than the Czechs for the seed cotton he sold them.

I overheard one of the hired workers complaining about the fact that our family picked the best bolls before he got a chance to pick in that area, and I mentioned this to Papa. His response was: "Let them complain. They sure would not want to do the picking the way we have to. Besides, our cotton is better picking, even without the few big bolls, than they could find in most fields which had not even been picked over before they got to it."

I had not given much thought to how so many little things determined how a crop would turn out until I did some of the planting. Before we planted, however, a short-toothed, light, two-row harrow was used to make the soil more pliable. Walking behind a harrow pulled by a pair of mules was comparatively easy since it required little concentration or hard work, and a lot of territory could be covered in a day's time.

Planting corn and planting cotton were a whole lot alike, but corn was normally planted two to three weeks earlier and the seeds farther apart. Both had to be planted with considerable care, and it was a job Papa would entrust to no one except himself, Shine, or one of his sons. By the time I was old enough to do some planting, we had a one-row riding planter that dropped seeds according to the setting on a disklike plate located at the bottom of the planting box. As the planter was pulled forward, a mechanism was triggered which let the seeds drop in a trench made by a plowshare mounted on the front

A Czech family resting briefly after emptying their cotton sacks into the trailer hitched to their 1925 Model A Ford, about 1932. (Photograph courtesy Adolf Vajdak)

end of the planter. Then a couple of plowshares in back of the planting box covered the seed.

As simple as this sounds, there was much more to the operation than that. The first step was to take the sacks of seed to the field. The planter box had to be filled each time before it ran out of seed. It had to be carefully watched, because if it ran out, a vacant space would appear, and I knew I would catch it if this ever happened. Every inch of land was precious, and it was wasteful not to use it for producing something of value. The depth of the plowshares making the planting and covering furrows had to be just right, not too deep and not too shallow, and had to be watched closely at all times. Also, Papa demanded that the rows be planted absolutely straight.

It usually was colder when the corn was planted, and sometimes it could be a cold job. If so, I could get off and walk behind the planter, but it also was more difficult to see if the seeds were coming out of the box just right. Since there never was any way of telling for sure, I anxiously awaited the time when the plants came up. If there was a skip of as much as two or three feet, I had to fill it in by making a furrow with a hoe and dropping each seed by hand and then covering it up.

Within a couple of hours after the corn or cotton was planted, we packed the soil firmly over it with a homemade roller to hold the moisture in place. Our roller was a straight and perfectly round log, selected and cut from our pasture for this specific purpose. After the bark was skinned off to make a smooth surface and it was sufficiently dry, an iron peg was driven in the center of each end. Chains were attached to each of the two pegs so that they met at the exact center in front of the log, at which point a singletree was attached so a mule could be hitched to it. Since the log rotated as it rolled over the soil, it was an easy job for both mule and boy, particularly since it was light, and I could ride the mule and cover two rows at a time. About the only difficulty that arose was when the dirt was not completely dry in a few spots after the planting. In this case, some of the damp dirt stuck to the roller and created a lump, which got bigger and bigger as it accumulated additional black, waxy soil. I had to get off the mule and scrape it off when this happened. If the soil stuck too badly, then I had to wait an additional hour or so until it was completely dried. Rolling the soil was a pleasant aesthetic feeling, seeing the contrast between the part that had been packed so smoothly and neatly and the relatively uneven soil before it was rolled.

When we planted a few short rows of sorghum cane or Sudan grass, we used a walking planter. It was pulled by a mule, planted one row at a time, and we walked behind it. The walking planter was lighter and easier to maneuver when one had to suddenly change the depth or cover the seed with more dirt. We also broadcast a small patch of Sudan grass or oats close to the barn so we could take a hand sickle and cut off an armload to feed the livestock and not have to carry it far.

In this case, the soil was first prepared by listing, which took quite a bit of time and skill to cover a small area. After it was listed, a regular harrow, weighted down with large rocks to make it heavy enough to penetrate the freshly plowed soil, was used to pulverize it. Then the seed was thrown by hand (broadcasted) in such fashion as to get it spread equally. Then the harrow, this time minus the rocks, was used to cover up the seed with a light layer of soil.

Even though it took a few days before the seeds fully germinated and came up through the soil to become visible plants, Papa went to the field every day to check on how they were doing. He showed me how to get down on my knees and inspect the planted seed to see if it was coming up. We removed the dirt over and around the seed very carefully so as not to disturb it in any way and then put it back and patted it gently. This was done with tenderness since every single potential plant was important. As a youngster, I did not really appreciate Papa's excitement at seeing the seed germinate, but as I grew up to participate in the actual planting, I realized how much it meant to him. When the plants formed neat rows of bright-green color, it was a sight to behold that buoyed our spirits and hopes for a successful crop year.

Since corn was planted first, it was up and well established before we started the cotton crop. As soon as it was up, our work pace picked up quite a bit. While the number of times corn was worked varied each year because of weather and other factors, each row received some kind of attention an average of about eighteen times. It was normally plowed or cultivated five and chopped four times. So growing corn involved lots of work hours, and there was no modern machinery or herbicide to make any of it easy. The Americans did not work their cornfields nearly as many times and were not nearly as thorough when they did. Also, unlike our women, theirs did not work in the field at all.

All of our cultivating and plowing was done by men. Thinning crops with hoes, chopping weeds, pulling corn suckers, cutting tops and tying them into bundles, and pulling corn were done by all family members, including Mama and my sisters. The men made shocks and stacks out of the tops, hauled the corn to the barn, and unloaded it. We did not use any hired help, other than Shine, in growing our corn, because we could better use what little money we had on so many things other than hired labor.

I began to help with the chopping in the fields when I was six years of age. But I felt more grown up than my actual age and was excited when Papa decided my time had finally come to do some cultivating when I was nine. I proudly left for the field, ready to do my first real man's job. Papa was wise to let me have Emma and Mary, our steadiest and safest mules, hitched to a one-row walking cultivator. With the lines tied behind my back and holding onto the handles that guided the plowshares, I started ever so slowly down that first row. Papa walked along beside me the first couple of rows to instruct me in the art of operating the cultivator as we moved along. I had to be very careful to cultivate as close as possible on each side of the plants without covering them up. But in spite of all care, an occasional plant became at least partly covered with dirt. Each time this happened, I had to stop the mules and carefully uncover it by hand, because each and every stalk counted.

As the day wore on, I got the hang of it and became relaxed to the point where I noticed a lot of little things. It was a quiet and peaceful time. The mules switched their tails at an occasional horsefly as they perspired when the sun got higher. The traces jingled a little, and the harness creaked. The wheels and the plowshares made a pleasant, soft soil sound. Occasionally, some of the soft dirt would roll up on the wheels and, if there was a breeze, some of it blew in my shoes. It really felt good to sweat since it kept my body temperature down, and I imagined how good each plant felt as the cultivator loosened the soil around it. And, of course, so much of our family's welfare was tied directly to how well our crops were doing that I could not avoid some sense of excitement at feeling I had some part in its progress.

By the end of the day I was tired from walking behind the cultivator, guiding the mules, and handling the plowshares all at the same time for about ten hours. But I was ready to go at it the next day, and walking behind a cultivator became one of my favorite farm tasks.

One thing I noticed was that our mules seemed to have a built-in sense for quitting time. They kept about the same pace all morning and all afternoon except when it got close to twelve noon, and again just after sundown. We always stopped plowing on the end closest to the house and barn. As the position of the sun indicated it was getting close to each of the two quitting times, the mules would go slower and slower as we went away from the house. But when we turned around and headed in the direction of the upper end, they would pick up the pace. By the time we reached the end of the row nearest the house, I would be trying to get them to slow down, and the lines would cut ridges in my shoulders and back. This is one reason that when someone says that mules are dumb I counter by saying that in some ways they are very smart.

Papa was a firm believer in getting as much as he could out of a crop, so we worked at it accordingly. While the Americans let suckers grow on their cornstalks and did not make fodder, we Czechs did exactly the opposite, without fail. Papa believed the best corn yields resulted from having single stalks about three feet apart. Consequently, we never let two stalks stand closer. When they got up to about two or three feet in height, some stalks developed offshoots, which we called suckers. If left undisturbed, the offshoot produced an ear of corn as did its parent stalk. But Papa felt the ear on the offshoot robbed nutrients from the other one and that one big ear was better than two little ones. Consequently, we pulled the suckers off by hand and fed them to our cows.

Pulling suckers was fun compared with making fodder. Each time I see a painting of a tranquil farm scene in which the artist has symmetrical and neat shocks and stacks of fodder, I cannot help but wonder if he ever had any idea of what a dirty and sweaty job it was to make those shocks and stacks.

As soon as the ears were fully developed, Papa picked a day to cut corn tops when the weather forecast indicated no rain in sight for the next few days. All of our family members went to the cornfield fully equipped with sharp butcher knives borrowed from the kitchen. Each of us took two rows at a time, cut the green tops off just above each ear of corn, and laid them neatly on the ground between the rows.

After the tops were left out in the sun for a few days and the dried leaves turned to a light-tan color, they were ready to be gathered together in bundles eight to nine inches in diameter and tied tight in the middle with strong hemp twine. Then twenty to thirty bundles were bunched together to make shocks that were left in the field for further drying and curing. Tying bundles was done early in the morning before the dew was dry and the air was humid. While this was fine for squeezing the stalks together to make a compact bundle, it also added to the amount of sweat and dirt that stuck to the leaves and ended up on our wrists, hands, and clothes. Also, small dried-leaf particles broke off and added to our misery. This was no job for someone allergic to dust or high humidity.

After the corn tops were fully dry, the bundles were thrown on a wagon and hauled to a place near the barn. Sometimes wasps found the shocks to be an ideal place to build their nests, a situation that brought on challenges for which we were prepared. Also, an occasional skunk decided to spend some time in a shock, in which case it was picked up later after it was free and clear. A center pole was placed in the ground, and the bundles were laid around it so that the stack became smaller in diameter with each successive layer. This part, too, was dirty and sweaty work as the particles of dust and shattered leaves

stuck to our skin. A dip in the stock tank or a bath in the washtub and a clean change of clothes felt good when the fodder
stack had been completed. I never looked forward to doing it
again the next year.

We Czechs believed in getting the fullest possible use out of
everything we produced. In the case of corn, this included all
of the kernels, cobs, shucks, leaves, tops, and even the dried
stalk itself.

As soon as the ears were developed but the kernels still soft
and milky, we picked out a few to eat, which Mama cooked.
And every one of them was good. The shucks and corn hair
from the ears were tender and made good feed, especially for
the cows and calves.

We broke off a few ears of corn before it was harvested
to give to livestock and to make cornmeal, because we thought
humans and animals alike deserved a break from last year's
crop, which had a few weevils. But we finished all of the corn
with weevils in it until it was all used up before the next year's
crop was put in the barn. Once in the barn, it was used most
of the time shelled, but sometimes with cob and all.

I must have shucked and shelled more than a million ears
of corn, one at a time. Our hand-cranked, boy-powered sheller
was an ingenious device which shelled each ear cleanly, leaving the kernels in the box on which it was mounted and flip-
ping the cobs out on the ground.

We had multiple uses for shelled corn. Some was thrown
in a wide circle among the poultry twice a day. We also carried
shelled corn in a sack to the gin, where it was ground into a
fine-textured cornmeal. We used lots of cornmeal, especially
for making corn bread, and Mama made a real fine corn mush.

The mules and hogs were fed with the kernels still on the
cob. The cobs were taken from the mules' feedboxes and saved
for other purposes, as were those left over from the corn sheller.
Because the cobs were so muddy and messy after the hogs had
eaten the corn, they were left in their pens along with the rest

of the debris, such as watermelon rinds and things of that sort. But these were the only cobs that were wasted.

Corncobs had a variety of uses. They were burned in our cookstove, in the wood heater, and under the washpot. They also were used for soaking with a mixture of kerosene and sulfur and then hung around dogs' necks as a homemade remedy for the mange and distemper. Cobs made good stoppers for water jugs, and if a cork was not available, they were good substitutes for fishing with a pole. A popular use for cobs was found in the outhouse when the supply of pages from the previous year's Sears, Roebuck or Montgomery Ward catalogs was used up. Although I would make no claim for authenticity, I believe I have a good clue to where the expression "rougher than a cob" originated. My friends and I found cobs to be good substitutes for imaginary baseballs. If the wind was just right, I could throw a tremendous curve or a drop and had a good chance of "fanning" other boys, who batted with the first stick they could find as a substitute for a bat. Corncob fights were another practical use. We got a lot of inexpensive entertainment out of cobs as substitutes for bought athletic equipment.

We were the only family in our community that had a corn crusher, which crushed the kernels and cobs together much coarser than cornmeal. A mule, hitched to the tongue of the crusher that went around in a continuous circle, did the hard work. We used the crushed corn and cobs mixed together as feed for young chickens and put a generous scoop in the hogs' slop each day, where it fermented enough to add some zest to the dishpan water and other items in it. It also became cow feed when they were being milked.

I do not know at what age I first heard the expression "husking corn." It was not part of our vocabulary, because we shucked corn, and the leaves removed from the ear were corn shucks. Even the corn shucks had some uses, most of them serving as feed for cows and calves. For some reason our mules would not eat shucks, even if there was nothing else edible around. We filled cotton-cloth ticking with shucks and used it as cover to sleep under in the colder parts of the year. Some kids even made corn-shuck cigarettes.

Sometimes we cut a few corn tops after the ears had matured but the leaves were still green to give the cows or mules an extra treat. After the corn crop had been gathered, our cows and mules cleaned up any leftover leaves and weeds before we cut the stalks. After the stalks were cut, they were plowed under to serve as a source of both fertilizer and mulch for next year's crops. Thus, every part of every corn stalk had some use, and even the weeds had some use.

Even though quite a bit of the work in producing cotton and corn was similar, cotton took much more of our time, and also the work was harder. Each row had to be gone over an average of twenty-one times each crop year. It was plowed or cultivated seven times, chopped five times, and picked four times, which included the final scrapping. I never tried to figure out how many miles we covered collectively, but it was a heck of a lot, and every inch of it on foot. It also was during the hottest time of the year and when the days were the longest. And Papa did not believe in our fooling around about being ready to go before sunup and staying in the field until after sundown.

Seeing cotton come up was a joyful experience, but it also signaled the beginning of about a six-month-long steady diet of fieldwork. The first chopping was tedious and took a long time since the plants, which came up about an inch apart, had to be thinned to about eight inches apart. This was about the width of the blade of a hoe, which in effect meant that we left only a very small amount of soil undisturbed along with a cotton plant. Since this was comparatively slow going, I occasionally paused long enough to gauge how much I had covered and how much farther I had to go on each row. But I did not pause very long or often because Papa did not want his offspring doing anything that might encourage our hired hands to do likewise. Papa expected a full day's work for a full day's pay from his hired hands.

Since chopping and picking between thirty and thirty-five acres of cotton was too much for our family to cover in such a limited amount of time, Papa hired farmhands to help us. Besides Shine, our year-round worker, and his common-law wife, Lizzie, the other hired hands were a mixture of "Americans," blacks, and Mexicans. I do not recall our ever hiring Czechs to chop or pick cotton, and that probably was because they could not spare the time from their own farms.

Papa expected our hired hands to begin chopping at daybreak, with about an hour off for dinner (the noon meal), and to continue until just after sundown. He began the day with them at a fast pace, which they knew they were expected to follow. If Papa was not available, then Shine and Lizzie instinctively knew they were supposed to be the pacesetters. The hired hands provided their own hoes, but we furnished the files so their blades could be sharpened as often as they wished.

Today's young farmers will find it hard to believe that the going wage in the early 1930s for cotton chopping in our community was fifty cents a day. But we also provided them with a free noon meal.

Fixing dinner for fifteen or twenty workers, in addition to our family of seven, took a lot of food and preparations. Mama and my sisters quit chopping around 9:30 and headed for the house. I did not envy them for being able to quit sooner than I when I thought about what they had to do. They wasted no time but started peeling potatoes, pulling greens from the garden, shelling freshly picked peas, getting the meat ready, and perhaps baking a cake or two from scratch (there were no boxed cake mixes in those days). They also rounded up an odd assortment of dishes, glasses, and utensils (we never used paper plates, and plastic cups and utensils were unheard of then) and had them all organized and ready to eat by noon sharp. The meat usually was pork sausage we had made and put up in lard in big jars the previous winter, or some kind of chicken (fried, baked, stewed, or with dumplings). If it was chicken, these had been caught, dressed, and cut up that morning before we went to the field.

The kitchen was unbearably hot. With the heat of the cook-stove going full blast for a couple of hours, and of course with no electricity or fan to stir the hot air, it felt good to step out on the adjoining porch where it was cooler — only 98 or 99 degrees.

We put long planks on saw horses to serve as improvised tables under the trees in the yard for the workers. Food was carried out on big platters, and the workers helped themselves, always the Americans first, Mexicans second, and blacks last, and it was not necessarily ladies first in any of the three different groups.

As the workers got their food and cool water (sometimes even lemonade) to drink, they found a place to sit anywhere they could. Most of them sat on the ground, perhaps with their backs to a tree, or on a rock, stump, or whatever was handy. They usually sat in separate little groups of three, four, or five people. Regardless of the size of each group, the Americans never sat among the Mexicans, nor the Mexicans among the blacks.

Mama made sure that the workers had plenty of food so nobody would bother us while we ate our noon meal in the house. If the workers thought of something else they wanted, they politely knocked on the kitchen door, and one of us would go see what they wanted. They were never asked to come in, and I do not remember any of them ever setting foot inside our house for any reason.

As soon as they were through eating, they rinsed their dishes, utensils, and glasses in a big pan of warm, soapy water we kept on the back porch and put them in their separate stacks. If there were any scraps, these went in the slop bucket which sat on a pedestal on the wall of the house about shoulder-high. The bones were thrown to the dogs. But the scraps were very few, since the workers appreciated Mama's and my sisters' fine cooking. For most of them, this was the only full meal they got that day, and they made sure that they ate their fill.

As soon as their plates were cleared off and left stacked on the porch, the workers would lie down somewhere in the shade, wherever they could, without benefit of pillow or anything else but the ground. Some napped (Shine always put his head on a rock and fell asleep immediately), while others talked in subdued tones until one o'clock, when it was time to get up and start chopping again.

In spite of sometimes being expected to do more work for us than for some of the other farmers, it was a known fact that hired hands preferred to work for us because of the way they were treated. The good dinners had something to do with it. The hired hands knew that Mama and my sisters fixed the best-tasting food to be found in the whole Mound Prairie area. As we chopped along, even though they did not know I was within hearing distance, I heard remarks like, "Man, that was sho good eat'n," or "I wonder how Mrs. Frances can make her cakes taste so good. I ain't never had nothin' that tasted that good in all my life." I remember one of the Mexican workers saying, "I still like tortillas and beans the best, but these Czechs really know how to eat." One of the males teased his live-in mate by saying, "Sally, if you could cook half as good as these Czech women, I'd marry you outright." But probably the best testimonial of all was given by one worker, who said, "I knows I could get more money iffen I was with the W and P and A [actually WPA], but no kind of money can buy that good a' eat'n." There never was any doubt in my mind about the food Mama and my sisters prepared for the workers far exceeding what the workers had to eat in their own homes even for their very best Sunday dinner.

In addition to the good food, another thing our hired hands liked was that we brought them fresh well water when they were in the field chopping or picking cotton. When I was perhaps no more than five years old, one of my jobs was to be the water boy. Since we had only fifty acres in all, the upper end of the cotton field was no more than a quarter of a mile from the house. My job was to draw a couple of buckets of water from the well and carry them out to the workers while it was still cool. This meant that it was at least slightly cooler than if it had been left sitting for a while. I did it two or three times each morning and each afternoon. There was a definite order in which the workers got their drink. There was only one dipper, so the water came from the same bucket, and everyone used the same dipper. But the American fieldworkers always got their drink first, followed by the Mexicans second, and the blacks last. I often wondered about the blacks' feelings about this system, especially when some of the Americans chewed tobacco or dipped snuff and rinsed out their mouths with a mouthful of water from the dipper first and then continued to drink out of it even though snuff or tobacco rings still were clearly visible around their lips. But no one ever said a word about it, and I never knew about any field hand ever catching trench mouth or any other ailment because they shared the same dipper. Sometimes as many as twenty field hands used the same dipper and got their drink of water from the same bucket.

Nobody in our community provided bathroom facilities for workers when I was a youngster, If they found a need to relieve themselves, they simply walked out in the adjoining cornfield far enough from the others so they could not be seen. As soon as they were through, they hurried back and resumed their work where they had left off. If they happened to be picking or chopping with a friend or in a particular group, the others picked or chopped that row along with their own so that the absent person could join them without losing any ground.

I do not remember our ever having any differences with our field hands. They knew that Papa expected them to work hard but that he was fair in every respect. Sometimes when one of our hired cotton choppers or pickers got in trouble with the law, Papa could be counted on to pay their fines and to let them work it off on the basis of the going wage. In fact, some of my American friends hinted that their parents complained that Papa treated his workers too good, and if they ever needed them at the same time we did, they would always work for us.

A few things still stand out clearly in my mind in connection with our hired workers, even though they happened half a century ago. One was that, when Mama and Papa wanted to say something privately about one of them who was in hearing distance, they would say it in the Czech language. Although I was too young to say anything about it, I was embarrassed by their actions, because I felt that the persons being talked about must have known they were the topic of conversation. But they never said anything about it.

One of Papa's heroes was Franklin Delano Roosevelt. Another was President Tomáš G. Masarýk of Czechoslovakia. These two had to be the greatest presidents up to their time and maybe the best these countries were ever destined to have. FDR earned Papa's loyalties because Papa credited him for doing so much for his country and especially farmers. Not only did he give him credit for bringing our nation out of the Depression, but Roosevelt also created the REA (Rural Electrification Administration), which brought electricity to our rural community for the first time in 1936 (when I was eighteen years old). As if that were not enough, under FDR, the AAA Farm Program and the Soil Conservation Program were established, and Papa felt that for the first time in his life we had a president who had compassion for farmers. Not only that, but FDR was viewed by Czechs as a friend of Czechoslovakia.

But as perfect as FDR was, Papa did not like his WPA program. This was a public-works program in which the federal government employed adult males at the local level to do various kinds of work. Papa did not object to that part, but he thought Roosevelt went too far because he ruined some of our day hands. In the first place, only those who did not have steady employment qualified, and Papa faulted these men as a group because he thought they lacked enough gumption to work steady. He was proud to point out that not one Czech in our community worked for the WPA. Some of the WPA workers regularly chopped and picked cotton for us. They could work five half-days a week and were paid an outrageous thirty cents an hour by the WPA, while we expected our hired hands to work at least ten hours a day for fifty cents a day. And besides that, we expected our field hands to work hard when all of the Czech farmers in our community thought that the WPA men spent most of their so-called work hours leaning on their shovels and loafing.

So Papa was not at all happy with Roosevelt, who he felt ruined our hired hands because they would have liked to have been paid more than fifty cents a day and with shorter working hours in the field on top of it. He steadfastly refused to pay more or to shorten their workday, and although he did not like to do it, he hired more women as cotton choppers and pickers. As far as Papa was concerned, though, women talked too much instead of paying close attention to what they were doing and did not chop as fast or pick as much cotton as the men. But in spite of this big mistake, Papa still thought Roosevelt was a great man and felt that anybody who voted against him just did not know what they were doing.

While the work connected with farming varied from easy to hard, none of it could match picking cotton for pure drudgery. The excitement of picking that first boll around mid-June quickly wore off and dimmed perceptibly as it went on for weeks and weeks and weeks. It was backbreaking work that began at the first streak of light and went on, five full days a week, until dark, and through the hottest days of the year until after several blue northers had arrived. A person who has never picked cotton cannot imagine how it felt to pick each separate boll by hand while crawling on knees, or stooping over each individual stalk, and pulling as much as fifty pounds of cotton in a sack hung by a strap on one shoulder, and the load getting heavier with each additional handful of cotton.

Snook cotton pickers emptying their sacks into a trailer before the cotton is taken to the gin, about 1933. (Photograph courtesy Reynalda Janac)

About the only relief we got from a regular five-day week of picking cotton between late May or early June and Christmas came on June the nineteenth, the Fourth of July, Thanksgiving Day, and an infrequent rain. While we did not actually celebrate on June 19, we did no farm work on that day because we empathized with the blacks, who celebrated the anniversary of their emancipation from slavery. This particular day also served as a reminder to us Czechs of the sufferings of our ancestors in Europe before their escape to America. Of course, we took time out to go to an occasional funeral and also to school after it started. Needless to say, I fully appreciated the fact that Papa and Mama believed school was too important to miss for any kind of work. But we had to pick cotton every day after school, which let out extra-early for that very reason.

Most of the field hands wore blue-denim overalls and jumpers, and one could clearly see the white salt rings accumulated on the blue material from the sweat that poured off their bodies. The cotton plants seemed to suck up the heat and throw it back at us, and I was especially thankful when Papa assigned me some other chore. These included being the water boy, weighing the cotton brought in by the pickers, and stomping the cotton in the wagon bed so none of it would fall by the wayside en route to the gin.

The amount we paid for picking varied with the price of cotton. In the late 1920s or early 1930s it was as low as twenty-five cents per one hundred pounds. An exceptionally good picker on a good day could pick as much as three hundred pounds, so he had a chance to make seventy-five cents on a real good day. But it was too much to expect anyone to pick as much as three hundred pounds two days in a row, because if one went all out on one day, he did not have enough energy left to do it again the second day.

I was not good at picking cotton. Papa delighted in announcing at the supper table that some young girl had picked more than I on that day. But Mama never failed to comment on other things I did well, so as not to hurt my feelings too badly. For a female to be better than a male at something like picking cotton was not exactly complimentary to me. But it really did not bother me too much, because I could not get excited about picking cotton.

Unlike the hired hands, we kids were not paid for any of our work, but Papa was more free about letting us have spending money during the cotton-picking season. After we sold our first bale and paid off some of our debts, we had a little more loose money around the house. Even so, we were cautious about spending it even if it did not take much to satisfy our fairly simple pleasures. After all, when I was about fifteen years old, a very generous triple-dip ice-cream cone cost only a nickel, as did a big bottle of Nehi soda water. Movies in the closest towns cost fifteen cents, and an occasional tent show that came to our community cost ten or fifteen cents. And for somewhere around ten dollars I could get a nice-looking completely new Sunday outfit, including shoes, socks, underwear, shirt, a bow tie, handkerchief, and a suit with two pairs of matching trousers. My brother-in-law recalls being the proud owner of the first pair of long pants in Snook when knickers were in style in the late 1920s and that they cost $1.26 postpaid, ordered from the Sears, Roebuck catalog.

At least a full month after the Americans near us did their last bit of work in their cotton fields for the year, we Czechs were still scrapping ours. While they did not feel it was worth their time, Papa believed in getting every little piece of cotton left behind by the hired hands, who by his standards were sloppy and careless about not removing all of the lint from the burs. Consequently, we had to hurry home after school every day to change clothes, eat a quick snack—usually homemade bread, fresh cream skimmed from the morning's milk, and jelly—and scrap cotton until sunset. One year we finished the day before Christmas, whereas the Americans were through before Thanksgiving.

As soon as the final scrap of cotton was picked for the year,

Papa (LEFT) and neighbor Frank Kulhanek proudly inspecting the stalk cut-
ter they made and owned together, about 1930. (Photograph courtesy Clara
Orsak.)

the field was turned over to the cows and mules to eat the cotton leaves and any grass or weeds that might have sprouted
since the last chopping. Papa was a master of taking advantage of every situation that might reduce the amount of hay
and other kinds of feed that we had to use. But the Americans did not bother to open their fields to their livestock since
they had plenty of pasture readily available and were not concerned about the small amount of feed they might use.

After the livestock cleaned up all the vegetation, the next
step was to cut the cotton stalks into smaller pieces so they could
be completely covered with dirt when the land was broken in
preparation for the next year's crop. Our stalk cutter, which

Papa made, had five heavy steel blades mounted on a center pipe that rotated forward and cut the stalks about every eight inches apart. It covered two rows at a time and was a comparatively light load for a mule to pull. I enjoyed this task partly because I had the option of either riding the mule or walking behind the stalk cutter. Another reason it was not too bad a job was that it was a pleasant feeling just to know that with the stalks destroyed, there would not be any more cotton to be picked for at least another six months. This respite from the hardest and most tedious farm work of all was most welcomed by everybody in our household.

4.

Close and Cooperative Relationships

Personal relationships among us Czechs were closer and more solidly entrenched than they were among the Americans who lived near us in the 1920s and 1930s. And this difference was obvious to both groups. If a Czech and an American youngster got in an argument, there was never any doubt about who would be backed by the Czechs, but this was not always true for the Americans. This is not to say they did not care for each other. It was just that the ties that bound us together were stronger and on a more personal basis.

I have often reflected on the question of why our relationships were so close. An obvious answer is that our parents trained us to think in these terms, just as a youngster is potty-trained or a dog is taught obedience. The bases for their actions were historical.

Loyalty to one's family and kin was a carryover from the Old Country. Our European ancestors endured many hardships, which led to a certain type of closeness that comes from sharing the same kinds of adverse experiences. The fact that they were viewed as dumb greenhorns in the new country also served to intensify their feelings of closeness. Even in our community, the Americans did not call us Czechs, but, instead, Bohemians. It was a designation we deeply resented. I never knew if they did it because they meant to be derogatory or if they just did not know any better, but I suspected it was their way of putting us down. Papa said it was because they knew we were better than they were, and this was their way of getting back at us. Whatever the reason may have been, the designation definitely stuck and we did not like it.

We felt that being called Bohemians was degrading because it put us in a category comparable to uncouth, free-living gypsies. Since our ancestors were from Moravia and not Bohemia, we were taught that Moravians were better than Bohemians. Thus, to be called Bohemians was even worse than Texans visiting in Europe or some other country and being called Arkies, Okies, or New Yorkers. At any rate, we did not like to be called Bohemians, and it served to strengthen our feelings toward all of our fellow Czechs.

The Americans intermarried with persons of different stock well before the 1920s, which tended to break down their loyalties to each other. On the other hand, we remained pure Czechs much longer. All of my grandparents and step-grandparents were Czechs. All ten of Mama's and Papa's brothers and sisters and two stepbrothers who lived to marriage age married Czechs, except one. That one ended in a divorce in the days when divorces were very rare and carried a stigma, and they had no children. I often wondered if the fact that his wife was a non-Czech did not play a big part in causing the divorce. Thus the traditional ways of doing things were perpetuated through continual intermarriage and remained more intact among us Czechs than they did among the Americans.

Another factor that contributed to the preservation of our close relationships was that we were self-sufficient dirt farmers as opposed to our American neighbors and their less intensive agricultural pursuits. This situation called for close cooperation among all family members and working together as a team on an around-the-clock basis. We spent lots of time together, shared our experiences, and had few secrets that were kept from each other. With us, it was more of a one-for-all-and-all-for-one situation.

Since we Czechs were so imbued with what was called the work ethic, we spent many hours on our farm together and had little spare time to be with others outside our immediate family. Mama did not belong to a bridge club. She could not have played bridge even if she had known how because there were no recreational activities where women could have spent some time away from their families. Even if there had been, Mama, like other women of her age in our community, did not drive a car. To have to be driven to and from a social occasion would have taken at least one other family member away from something else that needed to be done. Besides, Mama had so much cooking, sewing, washing, working in the fields, and other things to do that she would not have had the time to go to anything but communitywide affairs which were attended by her entire family.

Papa was a community leader. He was a school-board member and held offices in the Beef Club, the SPJST, the RVOS, the Cemetery Association, the Snook Brethren Church, and the local cooperative gin. But he almost never missed a meal at home. If a meeting caused him to be running late, we all had to wait to eat until he got home. What's more, we were not permitted to have any kind of presupper snack or to taste anything until Papa got home and we all ate together. And we kids did not dare complain about being too hungry to wait until Papa got home.

Like Mama and Papa, we kids had no organized recreational activities for youth, simply because they were not needed. Our time was fully occupied on the farm working with our family members unless we were in school. So we had a lot of togetherness.

Even after we worked all day in the fields and ate three meals together, all of us spent an hour or two together in our parlor after supper. The reason we were in the parlor was that it was the only room in which we had a light. In the late 1920s, Papa bought a new kind of lamp which was simply marvelous compared with the regular kerosene lamps. It was powered by a mixture of regular automobile gasoline and air which was pro-

The Snook SPJST hall building committee on the front steps of the remodeled building in 1935. Papa is third from the right, front row. (Photograph courtesy Ella Orsak)

vided by a small pump operated by hand. Instead of a wick it had mantles, which were made out of a special type of fabric, glowed brightly, and made at least ten times more light than a kerosene lamp. Since we had only one, it was moved after supper from the dining room to the parlor, where it hung from a hook screwed into the middle of the ceiling. The rest of the house remained dark in order to save kerosene, even though kerosene cost only about a nickel a gallon.

Before we bought a phonograph and radio, our conversations in the front room were continuous, lively, and punctuated with friendly exchanges and opinions about a variety of subjects. If someone in the community got a letter from relatives in Czechoslovakia telling about how rough things were there, we talked about how lucky we were to be in America. Or maybe we speculated that some woman in the community was with child since she had not been seen in public for a while. Once a woman's physical appearance revealed that she was expecting, she seldom left the house. If she went for a ride in a car with her husband, she did not get out of the car where people could view her condition. There was no such thing as maternity clothes then, and the women did look rather unsightly, since their tight dresses accentuated their condition. Our conversations were about almost anything one can think of, with one exception—human sexuality. I cannot remember anybody ever saying it was a forbidden topic. It just did not come up in our family's conversation.

I do not know what kind of advice parents were being given about talking to their children about sex when I was a youngster. But my parents never directly mentioned anything about it to me. About the closest we ever came to referring to the subject was when I was about eleven or twelve years old and had begun to show some interest in girls. When Mama and I were alone, she hesitatingly mentioned that she wished I would not ever go with a girl that I would not want to marry. As indirect as this statement was, both she and I knew what it meant. I shuffled my feet, and my face turned red with embarrassment because Mama had brought up the subject. Somehow or other, I managed a reply something to the effect that I would not, and we both knew that was the end of any discussion we would ever have about the topic. So my human-sexuality knowledge was obtained from boyhood friends, most of which knowledge I have come to believe in later years was greatly exaggerated. Even after all of us left home, and to this very day, none of our family members has ever brought up the topic of sex in conversations with each other.

One of the things that stands out in my mind about our family conversations is the gentleness and kindness of Mama's remarks when it came to people. Papa believed in telling it like it was, but Mama was the opposite. If someone started to make a critical remark about a person, Mama very gently reminded us that everybody had some good qualities, and if we could not say anything good about them, then it probably was not worth saying. I have often thought about how my views turned out to be a mixture of Papa's and Mama's. Papa taught us to work hard and to try to be somebody. Mama taught us that it was not worth trying to be somebody if we had to step on people or run a person down in the process.

When we got together after supper, we did not just talk, since there were plenty of things to be done. My sisters usually embroidered or did some hand sewing; Mama patched clothes and darned socks; Papa repaired something; and we boys did something useful like putting neat's-foot oil on a baseball glove and getting it in shape for the next Sunday afternoon's baseball game, or perhaps shining our only pairs of Sunday shoes.

Some nights we cranked up our phonograph and played records. The phonograph was so small it could be folded up and carried around like a little suitcase, but it provided many hours of entertainment. We had twenty or thirty records, which were played over and over and over; most of them were Czech polkas and waltzes. Tunes like "Green Meadow Waltz" ("Louka Zelená") and "Red Wine Polka" ("Červené Víno") were Mama's and Papa's favorites, along with the Czech national anthem, which was sung in the native language. My favorites were Guy Lombardo and other big-name dance bands. There also were "Amos 'n' Andy" talking records. We all laughed over and over again at their jokes, no matter how many times we had heard them. But there was not a single classic in our record collection or any country music.

Among the things I remember most vividly about our phonograph were how often we had to change the needle and how funny it sounded when it wound down and the turntable went around slower and slower. When this happened, we had to turn the crank again to get the record back up to its regular speed. Changing records, changing needles, and cranking the phonograph were pretty much a full-time job, but the pleasures we got out of it were well worth it.

We got lots of pleasure from another invention that came along when I was a boy. This was the radio. Our first one was a crystal set ordered and put together by my schoolteacher brother. Never having been mechanically inclined, I did not understand how it worked even though it must have been a simple device compared to today's sophisticated radios and sound systems. It did not even have a battery, and only one person could listen to it at a time, since it had only one set of headphones. It attracted a lot of attention. A number of people came to our house to hear it work and marveled at what it could do, even though the reception was poor, and there was lot of static.

In about 1929, Papa bought us a real radio. It was pow-ered by a car battery, and all of us could listen at the same time since headphones were no longer necessary. This was re-ally something, getting stations like KPRC (Houston), WFAA (Dallas), and, when it was on the air, the station on the cam-pus of the Agricultural and Mechanical College of Texas, as Texas A&M was called then. But the loudest and clearest at night was XERA, broadcasting from Mexico and owned by a Dr. "Goat Gland" Brinkley. His main pitch was replacing male glands with goat glands so that men could feel young again. Apparently the operation was done for males only since I do not remember any mention being made of goat-gland fixes for women.

Since we were one of the first families in the community to have a battery-powered radio, friends and neighbors came to our house to hear certain programs. In spite of the fact that we had a wire antenna on top of the house, we were disap-pointed at times when there was too much static to get a pro-gram clearly. Some of my boyhood friends who did not have a radio were jealous of the fact that we had one but tried to hide it by saying that they would get one, too, as soon as the model we had was improved. Mama and Papa were especially happy when they got a "Czech Music Hour" program being broadcast from Temple, Houston, or even as far away as Nebraska at night. The announcers handled all commercials in Czech and played Czech records, mostly polkas and waltzes.

Mama finally gave in to another type of music in the mid-1930s when a flour salesman, W. Lee ("Pappy") O'Daniel had the most popular radio program in our community. He had a hillbilly band and advertised Light Crust Flour. But it was not just the music that Mama liked so much — it was Pappy O'Daniel's religious-type persuasive presentations. These were so good that he parlayed them into the governorship of the state in 1939. But Papa never was convinced that either O'Daniel or his hillbilly music was any good. He remained fully loyal to Czech polkas and waltzes until his death.

Although I liked Czech music, I was partial to big dance bands and such tunes as "Up a Lazy River," "Stardust," "Sentimental Journey," "Sugar Blues," and "Toot Toot Tootsie, Goodbye." We never listened to operas or long-haired music, but I believe if they had had Czech lyrics, then we would have.

One of the reasons our family relationships were closer than those of the Americans who lived around us was that we put in a whole lot more time working very closely together on a big variety of tasks. We were sort of like a championship basketball team — everybody doing our part to make whatever we were doing a success and feeling proud of how well we worked together. I would have been happy to challenge any American youngster living near our community to see whose family worked better together. I would have won every time.

This is not to say that the Americans did not do most of the things we did. But they bought a lot of their food, while we produced and put up just about everything we ate. Consequently, our situation required a whole lot more work by all of our family members. Some of the Americans did not make sauerkraut (*kyselé zelé*). So they grew only a small amount of cabbage, while we had over two hundred heads of cabbage to work with. Instead of putting up kraut in a few quart jars like the Americans, we put ours up first in a fifty-gallon barrel and, after it seasoned, transferred it to ten-gallon barrels and pottery crocks. When the kraut was ready to eat, a little at a time was taken off the top and the rest covered up with a wooden lid, cut to fit snugly inside the crock so the contents would not spoil. And none of it ever spoiled, since we ate kraut frequently all the year round.

All of our family members worked like a well-oiled machine when we made sauerkraut. The men cut off the cabbage heads with sharp butcher knives, carried them in our multiple-purpose washtubs to the back porch, and dumped them on the freshly swept floor. My sisters and Mama sliced the cabbage heads in half and cut out the pithy portions and tougher outer leaves, which were thrown to the hogs. All of us took turns shredding the cabbage, which was carried to the smokehouse, where it was placed in a layer about four inches deep in a fifty-gallon barrel. This was topped with a layer of salt. My job, as the youngest family member, was to stomp the cabbage-and-salt combination until it reached a juicy, briny consistency. After putting in some dill, I thoroughly stomped each successive layer of cabbage, salt, and dill until the barrel was almost full. I always did my stomping barefooted. By the time the job was done, my feet were wrinkled from the briny solution and extra clean. There usually were a few lighter moments when we all worked together in the process of making kraut. One time my brother commented to my sisters that I had forgotten to wash my feet before stomping the cabbage and had just come from the chicken yard. On another occasion he found a vicious-looking worm in the mulberries which had fallen in our yard and pretended that it had been in the cabbage we were about to shred. My sisters refused to eat any kraut on both occasions until Mama convinced them that he was only teasing.

One of the differences in the diet habits of us Czechs and the Americans who lived nearby was that we ate a lot more meat.

In fact, we had meat on the table three times a day, seven days a week. When they ate meat, it usually was beef, while we ate less beef and much more pork and chicken. Some of the Americans also ate mutton, which no one in my family ever tasted before growing up and leaving home. Another difference was that our food was much more highly seasoned, with lots of salt (which we bought in five- or ten-pound sacks), pepper (which we bought whole and ground ourselves), and garlic and especially onions, both of which we grew in large quantities. Still other differences were that we ate a lot more fried foods and did more cooking with hog lard and bacon grease, and normally our food had a whole lot more grease in it than theirs. One of my favorite breakfasts on cold winter mornings was fried homemade bacon and sorghum syrup covered with hot bacon grease along with homemade bread to sop it up with. My American friends used to say it turned their stomachs just to think about eating all the highly seasoned, fatty, and greasy foods that were a part of our daily diet.

Since we were big meat eaters and had no refrigeration before 1936, beef and chicken had to be used up within a couple of days after it was killed. Otherwise it spoiled. Pork was another story since we preserved it much longer, either smoking it or putting it up in a briny solution or in hog lard in big crocks. That is why we belonged to the Beef Club and also ate more pork than the Americans.

The Americans did not belong to beef clubs, but they were so popular among us Czechs we had three of them in our community. That was our way of having fresh beef at least once a week, and sometimes twice.

Between thirty and forty Czech farmers who lived within closest proximity to each other comprised the membership of each Beef Club. At their first meeting each year, two meatcutters and a bookkeeper were elected. Numbers written on slips of paper were placed in a hat, and each member family drew one. Each family was responsible for killing a head of beef (actually a fattened steer) in numerical order according to the number drawn. The freshly killed carcass was delivered to the Beef Club house, which was a small wooden building constructed for this purpose. The carcass was cut up in pieces by the meatcutters and placed in the same number of piles as there were members. The bookkeeper recorded the number of pounds and specific cuts of beef each member family received. These were rotated in such fashion that each member family had got the equivalent of a whole carcass when the cycle had been completed.

If the weight of the steer's carcass provided by a farmer was greater than the pounds of meat he received at the end of the cycle, he was paid the going price for the excess. A family whose steer weighed less than the amount of meat it received paid into the fund for the extra meat, also at the going price. In this way everybody came out even and had fresh beef to eat on a weekly basis.

Beef Club day always was a Saturday morning. Each family had a representative present by nine o'clock, and they stayed until they got their beef. Thus the Beef Club served the additional function of being a gathering place for visiting, catching up on local news, and, generally speaking, enjoying a visit with friends and neighbors. When a butchered steer did not weigh much, an extra beef was killed by the next person on the list and distributed at the Beef Club on the following Tuesday. But this rarely was the case. The member families normally fattened and butchered their best steers and vied for compliments about the quality of the beef they provided.

One of my pleasant memories about belonging to the Beef Club is the superior breakfasts we had when it was our turn to kill a steer. Each member delivered only the two halves of beef to the club house. So we got to keep all of the insides, none of which went to waste. Shine and Lizzie took the entrails, which they made into tripe. They also got the head after we took out the brains and tongue. Mama made one of the best breakfasts ever out of the liver, kidneys, heart, and sweet-

Snook Beef Club members in the early 1950s, waiting at the Beef Club house on a Saturday morning to pick up their allotments of beef killed that morning. This Beef Club had been in continuous operation since the late 1880s. All the persons in the photograph are Czech. (Photograph courtesy Clara Orsak)

bread. These were cut up in small pieces and fried in lard. Seasoned with generous amounts of salt, pepper, onion, and flour, they made a very tasty meat-and-gravy combination. Served with fresh homemade biscuits (there was no other kind in those days) and pickles, with generous amounts of fresh milk—this was a breakfast fit for a king. It was so good that some of our men neighbors and perhaps a son or two who came over to see how the killing was going ate breakfast with us. I suspected that they really did not come for that purpose, but just to get in on one of Mama's good breakfasts.

Since our family ate lots of pork, we killed five or six hogs each winter. All of our family members, plus Shine and Lizzie, worked at preparing the meat for our use, with preparations beginning the day before. Papa sharpened butcher knives and saw to it that the block and tackle and sled were in good working order. We boys filled two cast-iron washpots with water and stacked wood, kindling, and corncobs for fires under the pots. Mama and the girls cleaned the sausage-making equipment and assembled an assortment of pots, pans, binding twine, and other things to be used the next couple of days. We especially welcomed having a cold, fresh norther without rain for killing hogs and processing the meat.

We got up extra early in order to have our chores done and breakfast over with by daybreak. Papa picked out the hog to be killed and grabbed it by an ear while Shine and one of my brothers jumped in to help. They flipped it over on its side, and Papa killed it by plunging his butcher knife in the right spot. The dead hog was placed on a sled and hauled to a couple of vertical poles with a crossbar, to which a block and tackle were attached. The hog's hind legs were hooked up on opposite ends of a singletree and hoisted to the right height, where we scraped all of the hair off with sharp butcher knives by applying scalding hot water. Only the hair and outer pigment, scrapings, eyes, and the hardened part of the hooves were thrown away. Some use was made of every other part of the hog.

As soon as all of the hog was scraped and washed off, Papa gutted it and let the insides drop in a washtub. Most of the heart, liver, kidneys, melt, and tongue were put in a separate pot of boiling water to be used to make what we called liver sausage (*jitrnice*). The head was cut off and split in two so the brains could be saved for eating separately. After removal of the brains, the head joined the other parts in the boiling water to become a part of the liver sausage.

As soon as the insides were in the washtub, it was time for the women to go to work on the intestines. The small intestines were cut in about eighteen-inch lengths, scraped with a knife, rubbed in salt, turned inside out, and carefully washed in clean water. These were used as casings for regular pork sausage. The larger intestines received the same treatment and were used for casings for liver sausage. So we had specific uses for all parts of the entrails. The stomach was washed thoroughly and given to Shine and Lizzie, along with a few cuts of meat which they could enjoy for the next couple of days.

A fairly small amount of the hog's liver, heart, and kidneys was held back for frying and making a gravy which became the main dish for our noon meal on hog-killing days. The brains were fried separately and served with scrambled eggs at the same meal. After the parts in the washpot were tender, they were ground up in our hand-cranked sausage grinder and seasoned with generous amounts of salt, pepper, and garlic. This mixture was then stuffed into the large casings, which had been cleaned, and became liver sausage. Heated in the oven, or lightly fried in grease and served with sorghum syrup and homemade biscuits or homemade bread, liver sausage was a favorite breakfast for the next few days. We were especially proud of our liver sausage and always sent enough for breakfast to a couple of our neighbors. When they killed a hog, they gave us some in return.

Whether or not we finished processing the entire hog in one day largely depended on the weather. If it was to stay cold the second day, then some of the work was left over, and we did it at a more leisurely pace. If, as sometimes happens in Central Texas, the hog-killing day started out cold but by midafternoon warmed up, then we worked well into the night to finish it all in one day. Fresh pork meat spoiled quickly, and since we did not have any way of keeping the meat cold, Papa was not about to take any chances of that happening.

Some of the hog went into bacon (*slanina* or *špek*) to be cured by smoking and also in a second type of bacon which was put up in hog lard in crocks. Hams (*šunky*) were made out of other parts, either by smoking or in a briny solution in crocks. Most of the meat went into sausage (*klobáse*), preserved in two different ways—some by smoking and some in hog lard. A small amount of the meat went into pork chops. Most of the excess fat was cut off and boiled in a washpot for making hog lard, which was kept in crocks and used in place of shortening, and also for making lye soap. Smaller pieces of left-over fat and skin were used for making cracklings.

While everyone had plenty to do individually when we killed a hog, I was proudest of how we all worked like a team when we made sausage. Occasionally someone in our community mixed beef or deer meat with pork for making sausage. But Papa found some fault with it made this way, and only pork went into our sausage. Also, he did not believe in any kind of filler (such as rice), and he disliked sage. So we made only pure pork sausage with lots of salt, pepper, and garlic, and no sage or filler.

One of my jobs at hog-killing time was to keep a slow-smoldering fire in an old bucket which put out a high volume of smoke in the smokehouse for a few days. Using a combination of corncobs and rotted wood, if I did my job right, it was so thick in the smokehouse that a person could hardly see anything even after leaving the outside door open. Another sign of my doing a good job was seeing smoke seeping through the cracks of the rather loosly constructed smokehouse walls and door.

In keeping with our custom of making use of everything that we possibly could, Papa cut off the pig's bladder for me when I was about five years old, leaving a short piece of the tube attached. After the liquids were drained and the bladder was allowed to dry a couple of days, he filled it with air by mouth. With the tube tied securely with string to hold as much air as possible, the dried bladder was my substitute for a basketball. Even though it was smaller and did not have as much bounce as a real basketball, it beat having no ball at all. I won many imaginary games as the last seconds ticked off the finish of a big game by putting the air-filled hog's bladder through a hoop rescued from a discarded nail keg and nailed to the wall of our barn.

We were so proud of our hog meat that we gave our neighbors a sausage, a few slices of ham, or some other pieces. I often wondered if a part of the reason for this was that we wanted not only to be friendly but more to impress on them how good our meat tasted. They, in turn, reciprocated, and we talked about how much better ours tasted than theirs. I especially remember criticisms about their using too much garlic or not cutting their garlic in small enough pieces. Even though we did not think anybody's sausage or ham could measure up to ours, none of us ever said anything to anyone outside our immediate family that could possibly be taken as criticism. On the other hand, we were sure ours was so good that they could not possibly be doing the same thing to us.

Another thing our entire family worked on together was processing honey when we robbed our bees at least once each year. While none of the Americans had bees, we Czechs saw it as another way to produce our own food and also to make some extra money.

As usual, Papa took the lead in robbing bees and processing honey, but all of the rest of us had some part in it. He looked weird in his homemade mask, heavy protective clothing, and big leather gloves as he lifted the lid off the hives while the rest of us kept our distance. He directed a steady stream of dense smoke on the bees with his bee smoker, made especially for this purpose. Sometimes my brother and I made a bet on how many times Papa would get stung in spite of all his precautions and how many curse words he would use when he did.

When he carried the frames in our washtub to the screened-in back porch, the real work began for everybody else. From there they were taken to the kitchen, where the sealed ends of the honeycombs were sliced off with butcher knives in order to let the honey drain more easily. These were squeezed out by hand, while two frames at a time were placed in individual slots located near the top of a big fifty-gallon metal drum, which we owned jointly with three other Czech families. Once the frames were in place, we turned a crank, causing the frames to rotate inside the drum. The faster we cranked, the faster the frames rotated and the faster the honey flowed from the frames, hitting the sides of the drum and then draining to the bottom. Also, the faster we cranked, the more noise the whole thing made. After the frames were drained of honey, two more took their place, and the whole process was repeated again.

I estimated that we had an average of between 400 and 500 frames to handle each year, so that meant repeating the whole process somewhere between 200 and 250 times. That was enough cranking for one day, and even the promise of home-made ice cream might not have been a strong enough factor to entice us to agree to crank the freezer for it. Besides, being around something as sweet as honey all day long lessened our appetites for any other sweet-tasting food or drink.

As with other tasks, working with honey afforded us a lot of time for conversation. It also offered my brother another opportunity to tease his sisters. One of his favorite stunts was to let a bee or two loose in the house to fly around and scare the girls, who were deathly afraid of getting stung. One reason for these fears was seeing what happened to one of my friends.

One Sunday afternoon when we had company, my friends and I were standing around by the back porch when the subject of bees came up. For some unexplained reason, one of the boys picked up a rock and threw it at a hive, which was probably fifty feet away. Immediately after the rock hit the hive, a bee stung him on his left cheek, causing his eye to swell completely shut for a few days. This particular incident caused a lot of speculation about the intelligence of bees. The bee picked out the one boy who threw the rock from our group of four or five, and it stung him on the left cheek. He happened to be the only left-hander in the group. There were, of course, many stories of persons dying from bee stings. I do not know if my sisters' fears were caused more by the possibility of death or by having some part of their body swollen and appearing unsightly.

Perhaps the most unpleasant aspect of working with bees and honey was getting so much of the honey on both ourselves and everything around us. For those who have never experienced it, it would be difficult to imagine how sticky everything got. Even though we were careful, within an hour after activities started in the kitchen, we had to admit defeat. And the longer we worked, the stickier things grew — the floor, our shoes, cabinet space, hands, face, and hair. It was such a relief to bathe and get the sticky honey off our bodies that no one complained about taking an extra bath in between the usual Saturdays.

As the youngest member in our family, I normally had the dubious honor of being the last one to take a bath. Just having to sit cross-legged in our all-purpose washtub would not have been too bad, but I had to bathe in fifth-hand water. Since we were careful about the amount of water used and it would have been difficult to heat enough on our stove to have each individual start off all over again, the first one to bathe had the biggest advantage. Somewhere along the line, someone decided that kids were to bathe in order of our age, by sex. So my oldest sister was first, this being one of very few things in which girls went first before boys in our household. This meant that she started out with clean water. When she was through, next in order was my younger sister, and then the boys in order of age. Each one added a little hot water. This meant that, although I had the advantage of having the most water and the biggest accumulation of soapsuds, I also had the dirtiest water. Little wonder that after all four of my brothers and sisters washed off all of their honey, I still felt a little on the sticky side even after I had bathed. But taking a bath to get the honey cleaned off was better than bathing in the winter months. We robbed our bees only in the warmer parts of the year, so at least the air was not so frigid.

Normally we had more honey than we could eat before collecting it again. We gave a few of our best friends and neighbors about a pint each and sold several half-gallons, usually for twenty cents to Czechs and a quarter to anybody else.

Honey put up in jars normally crystallized into a thick, whitelike sugar well before time to rob the bees again. Unlike my children and grandchildren today, who would turn up their noses at the thought of eating honey after it reached this state, we had no problem with this. We simply put the jar in a pan of water and heated it until the sugar melted. It did not affect the taste at all.

Honey had other uses than eating it in raw form. We used honey for medicinal purposes, particularly for colds, coughs, and the flu. When one of us felt the flu coming on, the first remedy tried was a mixture of honey, boiling hot water, fresh lemon juice, a wholesome shot of whiskey, and sugar gulped down before going to sleep. It had a soothing effect, and we usually woke up the next morning with all of the cold or flu symptoms gone. Papa also bought a strong pine-tar liquid mixture, called Pinex. He mixed about one part medicine with three parts honey, and we took it for a cough. Although the pine-tar taste was not anything to be pleased about, it did a good job of curing our coughs.

These were, of course, just a few of our home remedies. A mixture of fried onions, turpentine, and hog lard spread on a warm cloth and tightly wrapped around one's neck was good for a sore throat, and a tablespoon of pure honey also was thought to be helpful. Sometimes a mixture of hog lard and mustard was used as a poultice for chest colds and was thought to be good for warding off pneumonia. Other treatments for chest colds included poultices made of a mixture of beef tallow and kerosene placed on a flannel cloth, or onion sauteed in bacon grease and flour. Heated cornmeal and salt placed on a cloth and pressed against an aching spot was used to relieve pain, including a toothache. Earaches were treated by rolling up a strip of paper in the shape of a funnel, sticking the small end in the aching ear, and lighting it with a match so the smoke was drawn into the ear. If no other medicine was readily available, flour browned in a skillet was taken for an upset stomach. If one stepped on a rusty nail that penetrated the skin, then a piece of bacon tied in place next to the wound was supposed to prevent it from festering or swelling. Other home remedies used by some in our community were snuff or tobacco juice on a bee or wasp sting and soaking a snakebite in kerosene.

Our family did not use many home remedies, because Papa believed more in store-bought medicines, liniments, and salves, especially those stocked by the Watkins or Raleigh man who stopped at our house about once a month. The "sales representatives" of the Watkins Company and the Raleigh Company drove panel trucks on regular routes through rural areas and sold all manner of medicinal products, as well as spices and flavorings. Mama was very partial to their lemon and vanilla extracts.

Also, Papa seldom fell for any of the products peddled by the medicine shows that came through our community. We never failed to go to a free medicine show and enjoy the entertainment, but rarely did we buy any of the products touted to cure every ache, pain, or disease. Papa was the first to point out that it was mostly the Americans who bought that stuff and not the Czechs.

We did lots of other things that did not involve the entire family but called for most of us to work together like a team. Some tasks were looked upon as women's work and others as men's work. Nevertheless, sometimes we boys and Papa pitched in and helped the women, and likewise sometimes Mama and the girls helped us.

Putting up jellies, preserves, and pickles and canning foods were mainly done by women, but usually with the help of some of us men. Sometimes the entire family picked berries, but not always. We boys helped the women pick the cucumbers, dill, onions, and green tomatoes they needed for making a sour-sweet relish called chowchow and for making pickles. We also got the empty jars out of the smokehouse, tightened the lids on the jars, carried them to the smokehouse when they were filled, and put them on the shelves.

Papa and my brothers managed to avoid getting involved in doing what normally was women's work better than I. Probably because I was the baby and was not of much help in doing heavier men's work, I started helping Mama and my sisters as a four- or five-year-old. And it carried over until I left home.

Churning butter was one thing I did that was considered women's work. This is something even a four-year-old could do. All it took was a constant stroke and patience to manipulate the handle up and down, which agitated the cream in a crock and eventually turned it into butter. Normally, it took just a few minutes, but it seemed much longer. To take my mind off the drudgery of the task, I counted the number of strokes and tried to see which of my two hands could last longer, my left or my right. But it was worth it when the globules of butter finally separated from the liquid and ended up making a tasty, golden-colored product that was its natural color without any additives to make it that way. Once the butter was churned, the cleaning up was done by the women, but it was my job to dump the leftover salty liquid into the slop bucket or in the trough for the chickens.

Another way I helped Mama and my sisters was making lye soap. Usually in the spring, we dumped an accumulation of lard, fat from butcherings, and bacon grease in our big iron washpot. Once a good fire brought it to a steady boil, Mama dumped lye in the boiling mixture. My job was to stir it with a homemade paddle until it was ready to cool in the pot. At a certain point in the cooling process, when it was about the consistency of thick syrup, we dipped gallons of the cream-colored stuff into low, flat containers of any kind we could find. After it hardened, it was cut up into chunks and stored in the smokehouse to cure. When it was ready for use, lye soap was about as hard as a storebought cake and had a slight smoky smell from being stored in the smokehouse. We used it in various ways — for bathing, washing dishes, and washing clothes.

Mama usually had an assortment of dirty work clothes in need of a good boiling in our washpot before they were rubbed on a washboard. In this case, lye soap, shaved off in thin slices, was, as Papa used to say, just what the doctor ordered.

Another difference of considerable consequence between us Czechs and the Americans living near our community was that we all made beer (*pivo*), while they did not. Whether the fact that most of them were Baptists was the reason for this difference I am not sure. But it would have been safe to bet that every Czech family in our community made beer and did not care if everybody knew it. As a matter of fact, it was talked about openly.

About the only time Papa took the lead in cooking something in our household was when it came to making beer. Mama was in the kitchen when it was being prepared and could not resist making a suggestion or two, but there was no doubt that Papa was in charge. On the other hand, for some reason I have never understood, we kids never went in the kitchen when Papa was cooking beer. Consequently, I never learned this particular art.

Papa made all the decisions when it came to beer making, including who had to wash and clean out the empty bottles from the last batch. One of the jobs my youngest sister and I had in this connection was making sure that all of the hardened yeast which had settled at the bottom of the bottles was completely removed. This meant cleaning each bottle individually by pouring a small amount of water and putting a few BB shot pellets in it and shaking it vigorously to free all of the yeast. This is one job we groused about to ourselves, although we would not dare to do so in front of Papa. We could not understand why the men who drank beer could not pour a little water in the bottle when they were through and drain the yeast out with it at that time. We speculated that, if they had had to wash the bottles instead of us, that was what they would have done.

Papa watched the beer closely after it was left to sit in crocks in the smokehouse, sampling it daily, until it was ready for bottling. One thing for sure, there never was any smoke in the smokehouse when it was ripening, since it would have affected the taste. We kids had to put the finishing touches to it by putting the caps on the filled bottles and forcibly sealing them with our hand-powered beer-bottle capper. Sometimes Papa misjudged when the beer was ready for bottling and jumped the gun. When this happened and the beer was still too green, we heard an occasional noise that sounded like a cap-pistol shot coming from the smokehouse as the powerful brew shattered a bottle and sprayed its contents, sending little pieces of glass flying in all directions. Each time this happened, Papa would curse and say something about knowing better the next time. I do not know which of the two things Papa hated more — having to buy a new bottle as a replacement or losing the contents before someone had a chance to drink it.

Making beer was something I never looked forward to, not only because I disliked cleaning yeast out of the bottles but also because I never developed a taste for the brew. When I was a youngster, sometimes Mama would ask me to split a bottle of beer. Since I did not like it in its original state, she put a teaspoon of sugar in a glass, and then when the beer was added, it foamed a lot. But no matter how much I tried, I never developed a taste for beer up to this day and have been accused of not being a true Czech because of this fact.

I have never seen any of my family members when they had too much beer or were drunk. Mama had perhaps a half a bottle very infrequently and never anywhere but at home. In fact, I have never seen either of my sisters have a beer to this day. Also, I never saw any of our community's Czech women drinking beer anywhere in public when I was a youngster. But the men were another story. Every time they went to Snook, it was standard practice to have a couple of beers in one of the two saloons.

During the winter months Papa often had three other Czech

We're Czechs

men at our house at night to play a Czech card game called *taroky*. In some ways it was similar to bridge but played with special cards different from a standard fifty-two-card bridge or poker deck. The men drank beer as they played. It was my job to see to it that each man had a beer when his bottle went dry during the *taroky* games. Even though they played as much as three hours each time, no one ever drank more than three bottles during the entire evening. I wondered if this was because they wanted to keep their heads clear for the game or they just got so interested in it that they did not think about drinking beer. They never played for money but used matchsticks and kernels of corn instead of poker chips. The way they carried on, though, one would have thought that big money was at stake.

I learned to play *taroky* and filled in a few times. When I wanted to deal a few hands for myself for practice, I had to be very careful not to leave any spots or any telltale dirt on the cards, or surely I would hear from Papa about it. He insisted they be kept in mint condition, and as soon as he detected anything wrong with even one card, he ordered a new deck from a Czech publishing house in Nebraska.

Papa normally put up about four cases of beer (twenty-four bottles to the case) each time, more frequently in the summer than in the winter months. As soon as the supply began to run low, I knew it would not be long before my sister and I would be called on to go to work on the yeast in the empty beer bottles.

Although making beer was against the law, local law officials were aware that all Czech families did so but made no attempt to do anything about it. In fact, they stopped by our house occasionally to quench their thirst. When they did, even in the middle of a heat wave, Papa closed the doors to the hot kitchen so we kids could not see what was going on. Of course, we knew that the law was having a beer with Papa, but we never mentioned it to each other or anybody else.

The Czechs in our community continued to make beer un-

98

til "3.2 beer" was declared legal in Texas, and the saloons began to stock it. At first, the 3.2 beer went over poorly, for the
men complained that it had a very sorry taste, did not have
any kick in it at all, would not even come close to being as
good as the beer they made, and tasted like something that
came out of a horse. But, one by one, they quit making homemade beer, and with it went a great Czech tradition, not only
in Snook but among other Czechs living in Texas.

There were some major differences in drinking habits of
Czechs and the Americans who lived nearby. Perhaps the biggest difference was that our men tended to drink beer at social
gatherings, while the Americans drank mostly whiskey or wine.
In fact, other than his daily hot toddy, I never saw Papa drink
either whiskey or store-bought wine when I was a youngster.
Some of the Americans made whiskey at home, which was
mostly for their own use. But I did not know of any Czechs
who did so. On the other hand, we made wine, but the Americans didn't.

The wine (*víno*) we made was not like the real wine that was
bought in bottles in saloons but was more like a wine juice,
similar to grape juice, except that it had a much higher alcohol
content than grape juice and tasted more like real wine. The
main difference was that we always added water to the juice
after we got it out of the keg.

Papa oversaw all of our wine making. We used wild mustang grapes, although some of the more accomplished wine
makers sometimes used plums or dewberries. We had an abun-
dant supply of grapes in our pasture, which we picked and put
in washtubs. Once they were brought home, it was my job to
stomp the grapes to get the juice out of the fruit. We never
washed the grapes, simply because there was no need for it.
Mustang grapes were very hardy and apparently resistant to
both insects and diseases, so they never were sprayed with any
kind of poisons. What few spiders and spider webs might have
been in the grapes did not bother us the least bit.

This saloon occupied one-third of the space in Ptacek's general merchandise store in Snook before Prohibition in 1918. (Photograph courtesy Ed J. Ptacek)

Once the juice was separated from the grapes, sugar was added and the mixture left in a crock in the smokehouse for a few days to ferment. When Papa decided it was ready, the liquid was put in a wooden keg and then withdrawn through a spigot, as needed. Water was added to the juice in different amounts, depending on who was doing the drinking. When Mama, my sisters, or I had wine, it was diluted a whole lot more than when Papa or my brothers drank it. Fixed in a weaker form, it tasted somewhat like wine-flavored Kool-Aid would taste if there were such a product. When we worked in the fields, our favorite midmorning and midafternoon snacks consisted of homemade bread dunked in a mild wine drink or homemade bread eaten with watermelon. One thing for sure was that we ate lots of homemade bread on a daily basis. While we had our bread and wine-juice combination, our hogs got what was left of the grapes — the stems, peelings, seeds, and meaty parts. As was typical with just about anything we did, nothing went to waste, and the hogs got an extra treat when we made wine.

5.

Brothers and Sisters

Even though we were a close-knit family and pulled together as a unit, each one of us children had a distinctive disposition. If someone in our community had been asked about us, he probably would have offered the opinion that all five of us kids were cut from the same cloth. But we were different types of youngsters in several ways

All of the children in my family had either Czech first names or the Americanized equivalent of Czech names. My oldest brother was Henry, which was Jíndřich in Czech. He was twelve years older than I and left home to attend high school in another community about the time I was born, so I had less day-to-day contact with him than with my other siblings. The one-room school we attended had only six grades. Since this was well before the days of school buses and it would have been physically impossible for Henry to live at home and go to a high school about eleven miles away, he boarded with friends of ours during each school year. At that time and even after I started school, the length of school terms was approximately eight months. The reason for shorter school years in my home county was that almost everybody farmed and depended on the children to help out when the crops were being worked and harvested. A few Czech kids started school as late as two weeks after the opening date and also did not attend the last week or so in the spring, because their parents needed them to help out on their farms.

A Snook Czech couple and their early 1920s Model T Ford in front of the car's garage, about 1925. (Photograph courtesy Adolf Vajdak)

Papa bought our first car, a Model T Ford, in 1923, when I was five years old and Henry was seventeen. Before that time, we went to town in a wagon. Going to the town where my oldest brother went to high school was an infrequent event since it ordinarily took seven to eight hours for the round-trip because of the condition of the dirt roads and the slow, plodding pace of our mules. So while my oldest brother was in high school, I saw him only during the summer months and special holidays, like Christmas.

After graduating from high school, Henry lived away from home most of the time while working in a drugstore in the county; teaching in three different school districts; being a partner in the operation of a store in Snook, where he slept in a separate room upstairs; going to college; and finally leaving the area altogether in the early 1930s to become an accountant with an electrical contracting firm in Houston. So while he was by no means a stranger, I did not have as much contact with him as I did with my other brother and my sisters. Even so, I knew him personally very well.

The main thing that stands out in my mind about Henry was that he was the Beau Brummel not only of our family but of our community. Although he was the shortest person in our family, he was a fancy dresser and bought and wore only the best of everything. This was good for me, because I got a lot of good hand-me-downs.

Mama and Papa stressed to us kids that we should look decent and that it did not cost a thing to be clean. As a result, we did just that, but Henry carried their admonition to the extreme. He was by far the neatest person in our family, partly because he was skillful at maneuvering himself into a position where he did not have to do as much work as we did and get his hands and clothes dirty. He never owned a pair of high-top work shoes or regular work clothes like those my other brother and I wore. Even when he helped us bale hay on a hot, sweaty day, he always was the coolest person and looked almost as though he had just gotten home from town and had not had a chance to change clothes. He even had his brown leather suit-case polished by the shoeshine boy in a barbershop in town when he was in college. Henry wore the latest young men's fashions and was the clothes pacesetter among boys of his age.

I remember clearly one incident that illustrates Henry's interest in being the community's fashion plate. Everybody in our community wore his or her newest and finest clothes to church, especially on Easter Sunday. This particular Easter, Henry had a neat-looking white linen suit, white shoes, a white Panama hat, and a brand-new red bow tie as his Easter finery. It so happened that that particular year an unusually cold norther blew in the night before, and Easter Sunday turned out to be a cold and windy day. We typically gathered outside the church to visit before services started and also after church. Before we left for church, Mama suggested to Henry that he would be cold in his white linen suit because it was made of

Young Snook men pose on the running board of a 1925 Model T coupé, about 1928. Note the bale of cotton stored under the shed attached to the barn. (Photograph courtesy Mrs. Henry Vajdak, Sr.)

such thin material. But he had to show off his Easter outfit and wore it anyway. I still have a perfectly clear picture of his body shivering in the cold wind, with one hand holding his hat on his head and the other hand in a pocket to keep it warm. He shifted from one foot to another while talking to his friends outside the church but refused to admit he was even the least bit cold, because his white linen suit was just the thing to wear.

Henry bought a wide variety of magazines and books and let his brothers and sisters have them as soon as he was through with them. He and his partner in the store business took me in his car to my first talking picture show in the late 1920s. It featured Al Jolson, and the name of the movie was *Sonny Boy.* I appreciated this gesture on his part, especially since he could have taken a girlfriend instead of his nine- or ten-year-old brother. Not only that, he spent as much as thirty-five cents on me for my ticket, a sack of popcorn, and a cream soda afterwards, which is probably more than his date would have cost him. I could not wait to get home so I could brag about having seen a talking picture show.

My oldest brother had a big heart. My siblings and I never exchanged gifts, even at Christmas, but he often bought gifts for us, and especially for Mama and Papa. Compared with most of the other young men of his age in our community, he was regarded as an educated person. His pupils in school thought a lot of him, and he had the respect of his elders. Even today it is not unusual for someone to comment to me about how they liked Henry as a teacher and about the things he did for them. He played football in high school, and I understand he was quite good, although we never got to see him play in a game. His first love was baseball. When he was at home one summer, he organized a men's baseball team that played against other communities on Sunday afternoons in a local pasture. He owned baseballs, a catcher's mitt and mask (but no shin guards or chest protector, which were not needed because a catcher was supposed to be tough), and bats. He was the only person on the playing field who owned a pair of spiked baseball shoes. He was very free about lending his equipment and extra gloves to other young men for a game, and everybody used his bats.

On a couple of occasions when he was part owner of the local general merchandise store, Henry arranged for me to get a couple of cases of soda water and a chunk of ice so I could sell soda pop at the local Sunday afternoon baseball games. With Mama's washtub and the ice and soda water, I was not only an entrepreneur at age nine but also the envy of other boys my age. I turned a neat profit each time. Although I did not think about it at the time, my profit really should not have been that big, especially since the soda water went for a nickel a bottle. Henry just made it look as if I had cleared that much money and made up the difference between the make-believe and real profit out of his own pocket.

We were proud of our schoolteacher, storekeeper, college-educated brother. Our proudest moment came when he was

Two young men pose in front of Fojt's store in Snook, about 1922. (Photograph courtesy John Fojt)

in a Czech play put on in our community by University of Texas Czech students. They studied Czech in the university's foreign-language department and put on plays in selected communities in the state.

Czech plays had exceptionally large turnouts in our community. People came even from surrounding counties to attend them and marveled at the students' abilities to handle the language so clearly and commented on how good they were at it. Before the play began, students were presented by the professor in his most correct and clearly pronounced Czech. When it was Henry's turn to be introduced, he made it a point to say that this was a local boy, and he had Mama and Papa stand up to be recognized as his parents. In these moments, Henry was just as much our family's and community's hero as if he had scored the touchdown to win a modern-day Super Bowl game. Little did it matter that he had only a minor part. A Snook boy was in the university's Czech play, and in our community that was an achievement worthy of note, especially since he spoke his lines in correct Czechoslovakian words.

Henry and I got along very well, since he saw me as potentially following in his footsteps — going to college and trying to amount to something. About the only thing I did that he did not approve of was deciding to enroll at the Agricultural and Mechanical College of Texas instead of going to his University of Texas. Through all my college days and for several years after that, he referred to the school I had picked as being for uncouth would-be soldiers and farm boys whereas his school was where only the elite and the accomplished went for their university education. He chided me about A&M being so sorry it did not even offer courses in Czech, when at his school he could take several courses in it. But he was proud of me for getting a college education, and I found out in later years that he even boasted that his baby brother was a professor at Texas A&M University.

My oldest sister, Ella (spelled and pronounced the same in both Czech and English), stayed at home until I was ten years old and continued to live in the community after she married. She was a low-key, happy person with a warm personality and a loud voice and laugh. On the other hand, she took offense at something said or done to her much more quickly than any of her siblings and got her feelings hurt more easily. So I was careful not to do anything around her that might get her dander up or hurt her feelings. She was a big help to Mama and fulfilled very well the role expectations of a girl growing up in a Czech farming household.

Other than being very kind, thoughtful, and considerate, the main thing that stands out in my mind about Ella is that she was an emotional person. She took the death of a human, a pet, or a barnyard animal much more seriously than the rest of us and also got the most joy out of something good that happened to somebody. She could not chop a chicken's head off with a hatchet, skin frogs' legs, or touch anything like that, and she was most afraid of snakes, dogs, and insects. It was her fear of things that caused my next-oldest brother to make her the prime candidate for his jokes and tricks.

One time Johnnie found in our barn a nest of baby mice so young that they were pink, hairless creatures whose eyes had not yet opened. He secretly put them in Ella's dresser drawer in the girls' room. Then he told her he thought he heard some strange noises somewhere in the girls' dresser. While he watched from a distance, grinning from ear to ear, Ella unsuspectingly looked in the dresser drawers. When she found the baby mice, she ran out of the room and refused to use anything from the dresser for at least a week after that. She also stayed mad at my brother to the point that he even felt sorry he had pulled the trick on his sister. As was usually the case, good-natured Ella eventually forgave him, at least until the next time he invented a new way to torment her.

One time Johnnie pulled something on Ella that backfired on him. Our family was getting ready to go to a medicine show, or a magician's show, which stopped in our community occasionally. Ella kept a box of fragrant-smelling talcum powder on top of the girls' dresser and usually used a little of it when she went somewhere. On this particular occasion, she got ready to put on some powder only to find that her powder puff was missing. Although he really did not do it, Johnnie told her that since our dog had not been smelling too good he had decided to put some of Ella's powder on him and had used her powder puff to do so. Ella got angry and refused to use the powder puff again. Since the store was open the night of the show, Mama made Johnnie spend his own money for a new powder puff for Ella, even though he insisted he really had not used it at all but only took the powder puff to get a reaction out of Ella. That is about the only time I saw a joke played on somebody by Johnnie that backfired on him. Although he was too cool to admit it, I am sure he hated to spend a whole nickel on a dumb powder puff instead of being able to spend it on himself.

Since Ella and I were the chief targets of Johnnie's pranks, we decided to play a trick on him to make him see how it felt. We concocted a story about sending his name in to a contest in which a free gold Elgin watch was to be given to the person whose name was to be drawn. We put a small rock in a box with tissue paper in it so it would rattle a little when the box was shaken and would sound as though there might be a watch in it. Our uncle, who was visiting us from Houston, typed Johnnie's name and address and a fictitious return address on it and sent it through the mail.

We anxiously awaited its arrival, in the meantime reminding our brother that he might win a brand-new watch. The problem was that we overdid it to the point that he got suspicious. When the package arrived, he announced that he knew about our attempt to fool him, because his aunt had told him what we had done. So he got the last laugh on us and kept us wondering what his next trick would be in retaliation.

Ella married a local young Czech man who was my favorite of all her suitors. Not only was he a nice fellow in general, but he helped me with my chores, especially shucking corn, before they got married, and that counted a whole lot with me.

I remember the weather the day they got married. Although just about everybody in the community knew they were engaged, I did not know when the wedding was to take place.

A buggy and the gasoline pump in front of Fojt's general merchandise store in Snook after a rain, about 1921. (Photograph courtesy Frank Fojt, Jr.)

It rained a lot the night before and all day long. Because of the muddy, impassable roads, Ed came to our house on foot for his intended bride. They walked about three miles before they got to a passable road that took them into the county seat, about twenty miles away. There they were married by our pastor, in the Czech language, but without any of their relatives present.

When we kids got home from school in our heavy-duty raincoats and rubber boots, Mama broke the news that we had our first brother-in-law. I was especially pleased, because I thought I had somebody that was going to help me shuck corn. Little did I know that this was not to be the case. After his wedding day, Ed never helped me even one time with any of my chores.

Our family was pleased with Ella's catch, since he was a local Czech who owned a garage in Snook. Anyone who owned a business like a store, garage, or gin was looked up to. And not only that, he had a house built for them attached to the back of their garage, which was just a few yards from the store in which my oldest brother had part-interest. Henry slept upstairs above his store, but he was able to take meals with my sister and brother-in-law. I ate several meals at their house, and it was obvious that Ella had learned a great deal from Mama in the art of fixing good food. She also was the first in our family to have children, so I became "Uncle Bob," a title I liked. Our Czech upbringing left no room in our minds for nieces and nephews to address their uncles or aunts by their first names alone or in anything else but a formal manner.

Ella and Ed kept a whole case (twenty-four bottles) of soda water at their house at all times. For somebody to have a whole case and for me to be able to help myself to a bottle anytime I wanted to was really something. And besides, they had a Delco system that kept the soda water cold in a refrigerator that even made ice cubes. That really was something special!

I got to play the slot machine my brother-in-law kept in the front part of his garage. On several occasions, when I was perhaps nine or ten years old, Ella gave me two or three nickels to try my luck. About four out of every five times, they disappeared in the machine, but sometimes I got two cherries and a lemon, and four nickels popped out. This gave me the choice of putting them back in or keeping them. Either way, I could not lose, so I usually ended up with no nickels in hand. I used to dream about hitting the jackpot, which sometimes built up to as much as three dollars. That would have been sixty nickels, and with that many nickels I would have had lots of friends and been rich.

Playing the slot machine with money provided by my sister was a good lesson in the long run. It taught me something about games of chance, which became a part of my overall training. To this day, I never have been much of a gambler or attracted by get-rich-quick schemes.

Johnnie (Jeníček), Mama and Papa's third child, was four years older than I. I never knew how they chose that unusual version of "John" for his given name. Given names like John and Tom (Jan and Tomáš in Czech) were common, and sometimes they were called Johnny or Tommy in their younger years. But he was the only person in our community whose given name was Johnnie.

Although he was named after Papa, their personalities were opposite in about every way possible. Papa had a loud, authoritative voice and could be heard a good distance no matter what the circumstance. Johnnie's voice was soft and persuasive, especially when combined with his other personality traits. He was our family's Mr. Personality Plus. Everybody liked Johnnie. He was popular with little kids, everyone in his age group, older people, and especially girls. In fact, girls his age used to try to butter me up just because I was his brother, in the hopes I might say something nice about them.

A distinguishing feature about Johnnie was that he was a natural-born prankster who always enjoyed life to its fullest. As Shine, our black hired hand, used to say: "Mr. Johnnie is full of devilment. He can charm the fleas off a dog." He got his greatest kicks out of teasing or pulling something on everybody — except Papa and Henry, who were the only exceptions. At the same time, he was the only one in our entire family who dared to question anything that Papa said or did. Even then, he used discretion at all times so as not to really aggravate him.

He was a whiz at thinking up a wide variety of things to do — from taking a bucket emitting a full load of smoke from the smokehouse and putting it in the open space under the back end of our outhouse when the girls or some of their friends were in it, to pulling something on our dogs and cats. I got so used to his tricks that I wondered what was wrong if he did not pull one on me for a few days. But I cannot remember a single prank that was in any way vicious. They were done just for the fun of it.

Perhaps the most memorable of all of Johnnie's shenanigans was one he pulled when he went off to town to finish high school. While he was still at home in the ninth grade, the Caldwell High School band director came to our community to give music lessons. On either a lark or a dare, Johnnie took lessons on a trombone from him. The director told Papa that when Johnnie finished all of the grades in Snook and went to Caldwell for the tenth and eleventh grades, he could play the trombone in the high school band.

Now, Johnnie was very good in athletics. In those days, there were no separate interscholastic league classifications in sports, and all schools competed for the county championship regardless of size. When he was in the ninth grade, he and his Snook teammates won the county championship in basketball, even though they participated against two schools that had the full eleven grades and indoor courts to boot, while ours had only nine grades and an outside dirt court. Since the basketball season coincided with the rainy season, our team did not get to practice as much as the city boys with indoor courts.

So in tenth grade Johnnie went to live in Caldwell to go to high school and, we thought, play trombone, as the director had promised. Since the band was to perform at their first home football game, our entire family made the trip to see him play and march with the band. However, instead of being in the band, he showed up on the field in a football uniform with the rest of the team. I was sitting next to Papa and could clearly see his wonderment, disappointment, and perhaps disgust at what his son had pulled. In the meantime, Johnnie avoided looking at us or acknowledging that he even knew his family was at the game. I knew Papa was boiling inside about it, and I felt sorry for my brother, knowing that he was going to catch it this time. After all, we had boasted in our community that Johnnie was a trombone player in the high school band and were proud of it.

Not only was Johnnie good athletically, though, but that must have been his lucky day. He played end, and another Snook boy was the quarterback, and they turned out to be an excellent passing and receiving combination. The first time Caldwell had the ball, Johnnie caught a touchdown pass. The home-town fans were excited and became aware of who Johnnie was and also who his parents and brothers and sisters were. Before the first quarter was over, Johnnie caught a second pass for a touchdown. The banker and some of the town's most promi-nent citizens couldn't contain their joy and complimented Papa for letting his son play football for their town's high school. Johnnie caught several passes and scored four touchdowns that Friday afternoon. After the game, people shook Papa's hand and bragged on Johnnie's athletic talents.

Papa's former disgust turned into pleasure and pride within the span of one football game, and Johnnie never did have to answer for what he had done. Unless it rained so much he could not possibly make it because of impassable roads, I do not be-lieve Papa ever missed any of Johnnie's home football games. Our whole family went often and basked in the glory by being next of kin to our high school athletic hero. This extended into basketball as well. Very few people in Burleson County, and especially Caldwell and Snook, didn't know who we were. And it was all because of Johnnie's athletic accomplishments.

The fact that Johnnie was so good in athletics got me in a bit of trouble sometimes. Since he was four years ahead of me, he played basketball in the tenth and eleventh grades for Caldwell against Moravia School, where I was in the sixth and seventh grades. Even though I had strong feelings of loyalty for my home community and school, I could not help pulling for Johnnie's team because he was my brother and their star player. But I tried to act like I was pulling for my school. In spite of all I could do, my actions gave my true feelings away. After one of the games when Johnnie's team had beaten us sol-idly, I remarked to our coach that I was sorry we had lost. He turned red in the face and called me a turncoat, because in spite of my intentions, he saw me jumping up and down rooting for Caldwell and especially when Johnnie did something spe-cial. Needless to say, I was careful after that about conducting myself as properly as possible around him, since he was also my teacher and the principal of our school.

I caught the brunt of Johnnie's outstanding athletic abilities when I went to the same high school after completing all of the grades in my home community. The coach had high expectations for me when he found out that Johnnie's younger brother was going to attend his school. But it did not turn out that way, and I suffered for it for the two years that I attended there.

Since Johnnie had abandoned the trombone and it was not being used, Mama and Papa thought it a good idea that I take trombone lessons. Although I never was as good at it as they thought I was, I played it in a local polka dance band and also in the high school band in town. There was a lot of personal competition between the high school band director and the football coach. They both insisted that youngsters in their respective programs had to spend a lot of time practicing, and their practice times were in direct conflict. So we could not participate in both activities.

When I enrolled at my new high school, the football coach took a dislike to me because I chose to play in the band instead of playing football. His disposition toward me was like that of a grouchy bear. Even though I did everything I could to avoid him, he taught my high school civics class and rode me unmercifully. My lowest grade in the two years I spent in his high school was in his course. Although my Czech upbringing did not permit me to use it as an excuse for my poor grade, I am convinced to this day that it was based less on my academic performance than on his dislike for me.

Playing football instead of being in the band without telling us about it was not the biggest surprise Johnnie had in store for us. He saved the clincher for just after graduating from high school. Being such a good football player, he had scholarship offers to play in college, and everyone in our family and community expected him to be a big college star. But instead of going to college, he surprised us by announcing he had joined the Navy. Mama and Papa and the rest of us thought it was a poor decision, but Johnnie's personality was such that none of us ever said anything about what we thought.

After spending a full hitch in the Navy, he wanted to re-enlist. He had gained more than his share of promotions, his basketball team had won the fleet championship, and he had been named to the all-fleet team. But even though Mama never said anything to him about it, he did not reenlist because he sensed she did not want him to do so. Later, when World War II came along, Johnnie was excited, because he now had a good reason to get back in the Navy. But that was the one time I can remember life played a trick on him instead of the other way around.

Johnnie failed the Navy physical exam. And on top of that, when he reported for the exam required by Selective Service laws, he was declared physically fit, and served instead in the Army, where he ended up an officer before the war ended.

Clara (Klára) was Mama and Papa's fourth child and a little over two years older than I. Even though she was a girl and I a boy, she had quite an influence on me in several ways. This was probably because we were so close in age and did a lot of things together. Being the two youngest children, when the others were doing more demanding tasks, even when we were five and seven years old, respectively, we were sent out to the pasture to find turkeys and turkey eggs or to look for our stray hogs. When we were seven and nine, the two of us had to drive our cattle, on foot, to and from a water hole about three miles from our house daily, including Sundays. We also picked beans or peas in the garden for Mama to cook and did a variety of other things that needed to be done by smaller children while the older ones were working at harder tasks.

We even got our haircuts together. There were no beauty parlors in our community, and our only barber cut both women's and men's hair. Bangs were in style for girls then, and Clara's haircut cost ten cents. When she was about eleven years old, a new kind of hair style was popular among some of the American girls. It was called a boyish bob and looked sort of like a boy's haircut, except that the girls wore their hair a little longer. When some of the girls in school had their hair cut this style, Clara approached Mama to ask Papa about the possibility of her wearing hers that way. I am pretty sure that Mama made a good case in her behalf, as she usually did for any of her children. But Papa's answer was a very definite no, expressing the opinion that boys' haircuts were for boys, and just because some American girls had their hair cut that way was no reason for a Czech girl to mess up her looks by trying to look like a boy. Haircuts were twenty-five cents for boys and men, but if they wanted only the backs of their necks trimmed, then it was fifteen cents. Shaves cost twenty cents. A shoeshine was a nickel in barbershops in town, but there was not anyone to shine shoes in our community.

We spent quite a bit of time waiting our turn at the barbershop, since the barber took an average of about thirty minutes per customer. Half an hour was not too bad, considering that he had no electric clippers or any other kinds of modern devices to help cut down on the time spent per person. But he also was a very talkative fellow who got carried away when he was telling a story to his captive audience in the shop. Sometimes we had to wait for a haircut two hours or more but did not dare leave the shop to go to the outhouse or for some other reason. If we did, we lost our place in line and had to start working our way back up again.

Clara was my crawfishing buddy. There was a ditch about a half-mile from our house that collected water and seldom dried out, which was our regular crawfish hole the year around. We firmly tied a piece of homemade bacon weighted down with a regular fence staple to a piece of string, then patiently pulled it slowly out of the water with the dumb crawfish hanging on and dunked him in a bucket of water. If we caught a dozen or more, we took them home, pinched their upper bodies and heads free of the meaty tail parts, pulled off the outer shells, and fried them in cornmeal. They probably did not taste as good as we thought they did, but that was because we were the ones who caught them.

Clara was a bundle of energy compared with the rest of our family members. When there was something to be done, she always tackled it with a vengeance. If it was her turn to do the dishes, she had them done in less than a third of the time it took Ella. She also picked more cotton than I did most of the time, which was a source of embarrassment for me, because boys were supposed to outpick girls.

Since my first school had only one room, she checked on my performance every day. Even when we went to a three-room school, we spent some time in the same room. And even when we went off to town to finish high school, she was just two years ahead of me. Clara not only was smart but studied and made good grades, being valedictorian of her ninth-grade graduating class at Snook. Everybody expected me to follow in her footsteps and do equally well, and my performance was always being compared with hers. So I probably applied myself to my studies more than if she hadn't set a lofty goal for me.

Clara was a sort of self-appointed guardian of my behavior, both in school and in everyday life. And she did not mind telling on me if I did something she did not approve of. If I got in a fight, did not perform well in class, or got called down by a teacher for something I had done, I could be sure it would be reported in the fullest detail. But I give her credit for causing me to think about the consequences of misbehavior in advance of doing something, because I would have been embarrassed for Mama to find out about it and apprehensive about catching it from Papa either verbally or physically, whichever happened to strike his fancy at the time.

Clara grabbed off more than her share of elected offices and positions. It seemed she was constantly hitting me up to donate money to a sweetheart, or queen, or some other kind of contest in which the girl who raised the most money (a penny a vote) was the winner. I did not mind too much, though, because I was proud if she won, and doubly proud if she beat out one of the American girls for first place. I do not remember her entering anything she did not win. One time Clara thought she was in danger of losing out to another girl who just might have raised more money. It happened that Henry was at home that weekend. When he was told that a girl with an Irish name might beat her out, he sweetened the pot to the extent that it was not even a close contest.

Although I thought she could have had her pick among boys in our community and even where she went to high school, she pretty well settled on a local Czech boy fairly early in her courting days. I felt that more boys would have tried their luck dating Clara except they were hesitant because of Papa's gruff voice and not too friendly temperament toward boyfriends when they came to the house. Although I never did hear him comment about it, I suspect her eventual husband was scared of Papa, too, but he hung right in there, and they were married about a year and a half after she graduated from high school. Like a typical good Czech girl, she spent her time after high school helping out at home until she was nineteen years old, when she was married.

One of the things in my future brother-in-law's favor was that he strictly obeyed the rules laid down by Papa about the time his daughters were supposed to be home from a date. One time, though, they stayed out beyond the designated time, to the embarrassment of her boyfriend.

One summer night, Clara and Charlie and another couple went to a picture show in a town about twenty miles from home. They got back well beyond Papa's declared deadline. Although they hoped to slip in quietly, it did not work out that way. We had a gate between our yard and crops and the small enclosure which held our mules and cows at night. Especially the mules were very cagey about slipping through if the gate was ever left open and unguarded for just a few seconds. Because they were late, Charlie was in a hurry to see Clara to the house.

But he left the gate open momentarily, and Kate and her partner slipped by and got into the corn patch. This started our dogs barking, which woke everybody. I still have a vivid picture of Charlie in his white suit and white shoes on a clear moonlit night running up and down the corn rows and yelling at the mules in an effort to herd them back into the enclosure. Mama and Clara stood by in horror wondering what Papa's reaction would be. He, Johnnie, and I hurriedly slipped on some trousers and helped Charlie get the pesky mules back where they belonged. I felt sorry for Charlie all the time we were chasing the mules, knowing that Papa was really going to lay the law down to him about never coming around again after this escapade. But to my amazement, when we finally got the mules back to where they belonged, he did not say a single unkind thing to him. I remember thinking how out of character that was for Papa and decided then and there that this particular boyfriend was looked upon favorably by Papa as a suitor for his daughter's hand. Even though my future brother-in-law no doubt was scared to death and embarrassed at the time, at least it tipped him off about where he stood with Papa.

I remember Clara and Charlie's wedding day as if it had happened just last week, although it actually was fifty years ago. It was a cold, rainy day in December, and the wedding took place in our girls' bedroom, because that was where our piano was located. Since it rained so much and the road to our house was impassable, the minister and his wife and Charlie's family members had to walk about three miles to our house in the mud, rain, and cold weather. I was honored to sing a solo accompanied by the minister's wife. After the ceremony, we had a turkey-and-dressing meal at our house, and then the bride and groom and everybody else not in my immediate family walked back to their respective starting places. Clara and Charlie had a one-night honeymoon in a town about thirty miles from our home and returned to our community the next day to start their married life as farm renters together.

I was Mama and Papa's fifth and youngest child. They chose the name Robért for their baby, which is spelled the same, except for the accent, in Czech and English.

One disadvantage of being the baby was that I did not get to do as many things with Papa as my older brothers did. When he and his friends went seining for fish in the Brazos River, they went with him, but I stayed at home with Mama and my sisters. The rest of us went the second day to enjoy a fish fry in a picniclike atmosphere. I did not go hunting with Papa as my older brothers did. When repairs were being made around the farm, they got to work with Papa while I usually was excluded.

While we all cared for and loved each other, I find it rather strange that, unlike people today, we never expressed our love verbally or openly displayed it. But we knew it was there. In all of the forty-six years of Mama and Papa's married life together, none of their children ever saw them kiss, hold hands, or even hug each other. When Mama's or Papa's closest relatives came to visit us on their vacations, not once did I see them kiss or hug each other. The only times I remember hugging Mama were when I got ready to leave for Navy duty and when I got back home safely. If Mama were living today and I could ask her why we never had open expressions of love, her answer would be that we didn't have to put on a show for anybody, because we all cared for each other, and we all knew it.

While our love for each other wasn't as overtly displayed or directly stated as seems to be the case with people today, we also didn't have shouting matches or major fights. I do not remember Mama and Papa ever having an exchange of words or speaking in a harsh manner to each other. I do not know for sure that they did not sometimes do this in privacy, but I do not see how they could have, because in a family of seven there almost always was somebody in hearing distance. Of course, it could have been possible that Mama was so subservient to Papa's ways of doing things she didn't cross him; but this, too, I doubt. But I do believe that I have lived to see a major change in these kinds of things, at least in how they were in my Czech community when I was a youngster and in today's larger society.

Another thing that strikes me as being different in the 1920s and 1930s from today is that I do not remember Mama or Papa ever lecturing us children about how we ought to behave. I assume this was because they felt they had taught us to know the difference between right and wrong and fully expected us to behave accordingly. Also, our parents never threatened us by saying that if we did something again we would be punished. If we did something once that was wrong, we were punished right on the spot regardless of whether it was in front of company or not. So warnings about repeated undesirable behavior were not necessary.

As with any other youngster, both good and not so good things happened to me when I was growing up. I still have guilt feelings about an incident that happened one Christmas when I was four or five years old. We kids always looked forward to Christmas. Papa and the boys cut down a big cedar tree in our pasture that reached the top of the standard twelve-foot ceiling when it was set up in our parlor. We did not have any bought ornaments, but that did not stop us from having what we thought was the prettiest tree in the community. The girls popped popcorn, which was strung on long pieces of thread, one kernel at a time. These were then draped horizontally, like ocean waves, at various heights on the tree. Little peppermint candy canes, pieces of homemade candy, oranges, apples, and walnuts also were hung at strategic places on the tree, which was topped off with a star made of cardboard covered with some type of Christmas paper. The fresh smell of cedar, apples, and oranges added much to the excitement of Christmas.

We traditionally went to sleep on Christmas Eve after singing a few Christmas songs in English and ended up with one in Czech, "Silent Night, Holy Night" ("Ticha Noc, Svata Noc"). Papa's voice was the loudest and Mama's the sweetest, and Clara accompanied us on the piano. When we woke on Christmas morning, Santa Claus would have come the night before, and we would open our gifts. This particular year I had my heart set on a little red wagon. Although I was not in the habit of saying prayers before going to sleep, I faithfully said them a few nights just before Christmas just to increase my chances of getting the red wagon.

But such was not to be the case. It had been a poor year financially, and Santa Claus's presents for us kids were skimpier than usual. I knew the size of my wrapped package was too small to be a wagon, so that was my first disappointment. When I opened it, my present was a small tin car no more than three inches high and four inches long. I then did a very foolish thing, even for a five-year-old. I cried and said something about Santa Claus not loving me. Mama and Papa, who were still in bed, took in every bit of my behavior.

My behavior that Christmas has been a source of embarrassment for me ever since, particularly after I found out a few years later that Mama and Papa really were Santa Claus. I think about it often and am ashamed about how bad Mama and Papa must have felt—no doubt wanting something better for their baby boy, who still believed in Santa Claus but not being able to afford anything better. This has been such a source of embarrassment for me that we never talked about it even one time in Mama's and Papa's lifetime. I have always hoped that they forgot about it, but it still bothers me to think that they most likely remembered the incident until the day they died.

Each year around Christmas, Papa bought a whole box of apples and a box of oranges. These were put on the back porch, and we were told that we could have as many oranges or apples as we could eat as long as they lasted. But we also were warned not to waste any part of the fresh fruit. These will always be remembered as the best-tasting oranges and apples I have ever had in my life. We were disappointed when the supply of fruit was eaten up, because we knew we wouldn't experience the pleasure of having an orange or an apple any time we wanted one until the next Christmas season arrived. Not one single apple or orange had to be thrown away because it had spoiled.

Another embarrassing incident took place when I was a youngster that I painfully recall some sixty years later. Our house was the closest to the school, and the teacher boarded with us. She was not only a good teacher but also an accomplished pianist. Shortly after she started boarding at our house, Papa bought a secondhand piano, partly for her use but also in hopes his daughters would learn to play it.

When I was eight or nine years old, I made the mistake of suggesting that maybe I would like to try to learn to play the piano. So Papa arranged for me to take lessons, which turned out to be a disaster. My friends poked fun at me about taking lessons because only girls were supposed to play a piano, and I turned out to be less than an accomplished pupil. After a short time, I wanted to quit but could not because I had been taught that once I started something I was to see it to the finish.

Toward the end of the school year, our teacher decided to have a piano recital, featuring all five of her pupils, the other four being girls. I made excuses about not being as good as the others and tried to get out of playing. But she insisted that I perform along with the others. She chose an easy waltz for me, which I never learned to play well. When it came my turn, my performance was miserable. My fingers refused to hit the right keys, and my timing was awful. Even my friends who did not know anything about music recognized it was a total disaster, snickering at just about every mistake I made. I almost quit before the end of the piece but struggled to the very end. When I finished, I got up to take my bow, which I was taught to do. Most of the people laughed while they applauded, and some of my friends sitting on the first row almost rolled in the aisle with laughter. I felt so bad I sneaked away to our car as soon as the recital was over without speaking to anyone.

When we got in the car to go home, my middle brother teased me about my poor performance. But Mama and my sisters made excuses for me, hoping to make me feel better about it. Papa did not say anything, but before the subject was dropped, I allowed as how I did not want to take any more music lessons on the piano. So my career as a piano player came to an abrupt end.

Something that could have turned out to have been an embarrassment for me, but did not, was smoking cigarettes on a couple of occasions when I was about ten or eleven years of age. Some of the American boys in our age group at school boasted to my Czech friends and me that they had smoked grapevines and corn shucks, which we had not tried. While we had more class than to smoke grapevines or corn shucks, we had to try something that went them one better.

Occasionally on Sunday afternoons when we had nothing better to do, I got together with our storekeeper's and ginner's sons and a couple of other Czech boys to play ball or do whatever else happened to develop. On two such occasions, we decided to outdo the American boys by not just smoking grapevines or corn shucks, or even doing something as unrefined as rolling our own Prince Albert or Bull Durham cigarettes. The storekeeper's son got the key to the store on some pretense and sneaked out packages of ready-made Lucky Strikes. We took these to the gin and smoked a whole pack in a short time. We really did not inhale, because we had heard that it might make us sick. But we had to prove to the American boys that we not only were as grown up as they but also had more class. We were fortunate we did not cause a fire and burn up the gin, along with different farmers' cotton.

That same summer, the ginner's sons got caught smoking. Their father made them smoke two cigars apiece while he sat there and watched them do it. They both got so sick that neither of them ever smoked again after that. As for me, I never took up smoking either and have been glad of it.

I learned to drive a car when I was about ten years old, because it benefited the rest of the family in a number of ways. While my older brothers and Papa were doing the more demanding tasks, I drove to the store or someone's house on an errand. Driving was not too dangerous in our community. Cars could not go very fast partly because of the rough roads and also because about thirty miles an hour was top speed for a Model T Ford. There was little danger of having a wreck, because when I first learned to drive if I saw another car coming, I pulled over on the side of the road until it went past. It was several years later before I was permitted to drive a car in town.

Among my favorite boyhood memories is going to the gin with Papa, riding on top of a wagonful of cotton. When I was about six years old, he let me take over the lines and drive the mules, making me feel grown up and proud that I was doing a man's job. In reality, however, little could have gone wrong because Emma and Mary followed the ruts without any special help from me. And besides, Papa sat right by me where he could have grabbed the lines guiding the mules if anything appeared to be out of order.

The best thing about going to the gin with Papa was that we frequently had to wait our turn for as long as two or three hours. He would send me to the store nearby with a quarter to buy us two big Nehi soda waters for a nickel each; ten cents' worth of cheese, sausage, and loose crackers; and a nickel's worth of candy. Today's youngsters cannot possibly imagine how much a quarter bought in the 1930s. We had one of the best and biggest noon meals ever, and I had extra candy left over to share with other boys at the gin with their fathers. Riding home on the cotton seed felt good, and I was happy to have had the chance to be with Papa and talk about things we otherwise did not have a chance to discuss because either he was too busy or someone else was around.

Another fond set of memories I have is playing in a dance orchestra with other Czech youngsters from my community in the early 1930s. Some of the boys' parents arranged for the band director in Caldwell to come to our community one afternoon each week to give music lessons on wind instruments and drums. Having at home the trombone my brother had aban-

Wagons loaded with cotton waiting to be ginned at Fojt's gin in Snook, about 1923. (Photograph courtesy Frank Fojt, Jr.) BELOW: Cotton samples taken from farmers' bales at Fojt's gin, about 1936. Cotton samples influenced the price offered to farmers, who had the option of selling at the time or taking their bales home, hoping the price would go up. (Photograph courtesy Frank Fojt, Jr.)

doned made me a logical candidate to try my hand at it. So I started trombone lessons at about age ten.

After we started taking lessons, the instructor suggested we might want to get together to play a few pieces of music and brought us some arrangements. At first we played religious hymns at church programs and occasionally other songs at community gatherings. When he thought we were ready for it, he gave us a few Czech polka and waltz arrangements. We enjoyed it so much that we added a local Czech girl piano player and a couple of older boys (also Czechs, who were about eighteen or nineteen, while the rest of us were from ten to fifteen years old).

Public dances were a major form of entertainment in our part of the state when I was a youngster. There were many dance halls, including SPJST halls at Snook and New Tabor in our home county and others in adjoining counties, which favored orchestras made up of Czech musicians. Snook was one of the more popular places, where they normally sold 100 to 125 tickets per dance. Only males paid, and the charge was fifty cents; women got in free.

An orchestra in the Central Texas area had been engaged to play at our SPJST hall for a dance one Saturday night. On that Friday, the dance committee was informed that a cousin of one of the orchestra members had died, and in respect for the dead person the orchestra had to cancel its engagement. The dance committee had to make a hasty decision about the scheduled dance — to cancel it or find a substitute orchestra on short notice. Seeing that there was little chance for rain, which would have naturally canceled the dance because the roads would have been impassable, and not wanting their regular customers, who came from as far as twenty-five to thirty miles away, to be disappointed, they decided to give our group a chance.

We were nervous at first about playing our very first dance for money and did not sound the very best. But as the hall began to fill up with customers, we got progressively better,

Snook SPJST hall about 1940, after it was remodeled in 1935.

particularly after some of the men had a few drinks and began
to feel good and complimented our music. We really put it together that night. A usual mixture of a polka, a waltz, and
every third piece a schottische, a seven-step polka, or even a
slower piece like "Up a Lazy River" was about right for the
crowd. By the first intermission time we were in.

Our orchestra played on a commission basis — one-half of
the total amount collected from tickets sold for admission. That
particular night, our share of the take was thirty-two dollars.
Divided equally among eight orchestra members, this meant
we made four dollars apiece, or about a dollar an hour. That
was big money for youngsters in those days. That night I decided my ambition was to be a musician with a big-name band
like Guy Lombardo or perhaps Wayne King.

This first engagement led to others, and we needed a name

for our orchestra. So we became "The Snook Polka Boys" for a while. Then we had a second Czech girl join, who played an accordion. With two girls, to be called "Boys" seemed inappropriate, so we changed to "The Polka Ambassadors." I do not know how we came up with the "Ambassador" part but believe it was adopted because one of the larger dance bands in our day used it, and it sounded kind of high-toned. As we got better and played regularly for dances and barbecues over the next couple of years, the type of music we played changed. We still played polkas and waltzes but shifted more toward what we called modern dance music. In an effort to sound even fancier, we changed our name again, to the "Lone Star Ambassadors," and billed ourselves as playing ultramodern music (what that was supposed to mean I am not sure even to this very day). We played together as an orchestra for two or three years until some of us finished the ninth grade and had to move to town to finish high school. But by that time, I had learned that I really did not want to be a big-band musician after all.

I look upon my orchestra years as a good thing. We spent a lot of time practicing and playing for different functions and enjoyed it. I enjoyed an extra amount of popularity because, in addition to playing the trombone, I was our singer. This was before sound systems, and I used a megaphone and used to see myself as possibly another Rudy Vallee. We enjoyed watching the pretty girls as they danced by and occasionally flirted with us.

One night we played at a dance at Taylor, a Central Texas Czech town about eighty miles from home. It was a special benefit-dance occasion, and a higher admission than usual was charged. The crowd was unusually large, and when it came time to divide, we made twelve dollars apiece. In 1933, this was more than many workers made in a whole week and sometimes even in two weeks. I ordered my first tailor-made suit of clothes and had some money left over.

On another occasion, we were to play at a dance in a little Czech community, Frydek, in Austin County. After driving all the way to Sealy, we found out they had had unexpected heavy rain that afternoon in the Frydek area, and the dance had been canceled without our being notified. So after a round-trip of about 180 miles and six or seven hours of wasted time, we had to dig in our pockets to pay for our share of the gas and costs for sheet music we had bought. We went in the hole on that one. There also were other times when we each made as little as fifty cents or even less, after playing for four hours and per-haps four or more hours of travel time. But it was all worth it. I learned a lot from my orchestra experiences and have lots of fond memories about them.

About the time I began playing in the orchestra I also be-gan showing an interest in girls. At first, my interest wasn't all that intense, but since the rest of the boys my age claimed to have favorite girlfriends, I went along with the idea. The object of my first puppy-love experience was a Czech girl in our community. We did not really date but exchanged notes in school and spent more time talking with each other than with other kids our age at parties or community functions. I never felt comfortable about our friendship, because her par-ents seemed to be sort of cold toward me. But it did not last long anyway. About the time things really got going good for us, a revivalist came to our community to organize a Pente-costal church. Her family left our Czech Moravian Brethren congregation to join the new one, and that took care of our having a closer relationship, for Mama and Papa and other staunch Brethren were strongly opposed to the new church.

Even though by the time I was thirteen or fourteen years of age I was in a school with more American girls, it was natu-ral that my closer friendships or dates were with Czech girls. The Czech girls dated Czech boys, and the American girls dated American boys. We were all friends, but when it came time to pair off, I was always matched up with a Czech girl. This continued even after I left the community to live in town to attend high school.

While I dated some non-Czech girls in later years, the attraction toward Czech girls remained strong. It probably was no accident that my wife turned out to be a Czech girl from a larger city. I lost a few points with residents of the community where I grew up because my wife was a Catholic, about whom they had a strong negative bias. But I gained more points than I lost, because, in spite of being a Catholic, she was a Czech girl.

Mama nor Papa nor any of my family members ever said anything about my going steady with a Catholic girl, but I knew they were not particularly in favor of it. After my future bride began visiting in our home, her humor and charm and good-Czech-girl behavior won them over to the point that she was fully accepted. I often wondered how they would have felt if I had married a big-city girl of Irish extraction who also happened to be a strong Catholic.

6.

Relatives, Friends, and Neighbors

While I was fortunate to have been brought up in a close-knit and caring family, I missed out on a close grandparent relationship, which was a bit unusual in my home community. Papa was an orphan even before he reached school age. Mama's mother died the same year she and Papa married, and her father died when I was about four years old. So while I remember one grandparent faintly, I cannot recall either his physical features or any specific incidents about him.

I was a little envious of most of my young Czech friends, because they had at least one set of grandparents. My jealousy was especially great when they showed me something their "grandpaw" or "grandmaw" had either given them or made for them, and they had close relationships with their grandparents. Even as late as the 1920s and 1930s, the kids in our community typically addressed their grandparents in Czech. Thus, they were their *staříček* and *stařěnka*. If they referred to them in English, it was as "grandpaw" and "grandmaw," and Czechs never deviated beyond this practice. That is, they never had any other pet names for them and wouldn't have dared think about calling them by their first names.

Grandparents were treated with great respect in my boyhood days. When answering to a question or replying to a statement, it was standard procedure to say, "Yes, sir," and "No, sir," or "Yes, ma'am," and, "No, ma'am." A "yeah" or just plain "no" or any other expression definitely would have been out of place and subject to being called down by parents.

Grandparents of children my age spoke only Czech and were not expected to speak English in our community. And they also expected their children and grandchildren to speak to them in Czech, not in English. If they were in a situation where they were forced to speak in English, then it was what we called broken English. I recall one such time when this occurred.

Once my friend, his grandmother, and I were the only people at their house. His grandmother was pulling weeds in the flower bed in the front of their house, while he and I were playing in the back. It was a nice, sunny afternoon, and we heard everything very clearly. A man drove up in an automobile and stopped before my friend's grandmaw had a chance to run in the house, so she had no alternative but to acknowledge his presence. The man spoke English only and said something to my friend's grandmaw. She was trying to say that she didn't understand what he was saying, or, perhaps, asking. Her reply to him was, "I don't know what you foolish." My friend and I both got a big kick out of what she said but never let on to her that we thought it was funny. We came to her rescue by going around to the front of the house and talking to the stranger while she went inside because she was uncomfortable around a person who did not speak Czech.

One of the things that was different between Czechs and the Americans living near our community was that as Czech grandparents got older they usually lived in a small house built especially for them within shouting distance of a son or daughter. Czech youngsters my age were taught to believe that their grandparents were wise and deserved to be respected in their old age, regardless of their physical condition, and were to be loved and taken care of. If they were in such shape as to require almost constant attention, then they were moved into the houses of their sons or daughters.

Definite differences between Czech and American grandparents of children my age were readily apparent in their dress apparel and in other ways. Standard dress for an older Czech grandmaw included a handkerchief, scarf, or bonnet on her head when she was not in the house, but not for an older American grandmother. Almost without exception, Czech grandpaws smoked homegrown tobacco in pipes shaped like little saxophones but never cigars or cigarettes, while the American grandfathers smoked cigars and rolled their own cigarettes. If they happened to smoke pipes, they were of the straight stem variety with bought tobacco.

While I fell short on grandparents, I did not lack for uncles, aunts, and first cousins. I had eight sets of uncles and aunts, all of whom I remember well. It would have been twelve sets, but Mama and Papa each had a sibling who died in infancy, and another aunt and uncle did not live long enough for me to know personally.

Only one uncle (*strýček*) and aunt (*tetička*) lived in my home community, so it was natural that our relationships were closer. The local aunt was my favorite, because she was the one in whose home Papa grew up after he became an orphan, and also she was my godmother (*kmotřička*). Being a godparent in those days meant much more than just attending church when we were christened and later confirmed as full church members. They accepted full responsibility for their godchildren in the event of the death of their parents or if they were unable to carry out their parental duties.

It was a pleasure to go to Aunt Mary and Uncle John's house. Aunt Mary never failed to have extra candy tucked away for me in her cupboard, and Uncle John let me use his BB gun any time I came to their house. Another thing I remember about my godmother is that she made excellent homemade chicken-noodle soup, kolaches, and pies and cakes. Aunt Mary and Uncle John preferred to speak Czech, so this naturally was the language we used.

Since my other uncles and aunts lived at least a hundred miles from my home community, I saw them less frequently. They usually visited us a few days each year on their vacations. Since we were farmers and it was hard for us to get away for more than one day, it was more natural for them to visit us. Sometimes their children came a week or so in advance of their parents to pick cotton and earn a little extra money. All of them were Czechs, except for one aunt who was an American (and also the only one to get a divorce).

My favorite uncle was a clock and watch repairman in Houston. Although he was born in Czechoslovakia, he came to America when he was young and handled the English language very well. He had done a couple of hitches in the Navy and married Mama's youngest sister somewhat later in life than was usual in those days. He was always laughing and in a jolly mood. No one could be around Uncle Frank for any length of time and not like him. He also was clearly Mama and Papa's favorite in-law and the champion beer drinker of all my relatives.

I have many fond memories of Uncle Frank, but the fondest recurred on several occasions. Mama and Papa were proud of the fact that their baby boy enrolled in college in the late 1930s. While they gave me all of the moral support and helped any way they could, they were unable to help me financially. So I was on my own, working my way through college, and every nickel and penny meant a lot.

On more than one occasion when I was running particularly low on funds, I thumbed a ride to Houston, which was normal for boys attending my college. None of us had automobiles in those days, and our main source of travel was catching rides wherever we went. After I spent a night at his house, Uncle Frank dropped me off on the edge of the city to catch a ride back to college. Every time he let me out of his car, he gave me a five-dollar bill, wished me well, and let me know I was always welcome. While five dollars might not seem much today, in those days my total room-and-board cost per month was twelve dollars. So this was kind of like having an uncle give his nephew in college perhaps somewhere between a hundred and fifty and two hundred dollars today. In those days

The sleek Model A Ford owned by the author's Uncle Joe, on a visit to Snook from Houston, about 1934. (Photograph courtesy Bertha Fojt)

I took my date to a movie that cost us fifteen cents each. The theater was within walking distance of her house, and I thumbed a ride to and from the campus. If we bought a nickel bag of popcorn, the total cost for a pleasant way to have a date was thirty-five cents. Another theater near the one we went to charged twenty-five cents, but we almost never went to that one, and my date fully understood why I preferred not to spend the extra money. When we happened to double-date, we sometimes ended up after the movie in a drugstore next door for an ice-cream soda, which cost ten cents each. So the cost for a movie, popcorn, and two large ice-cream sodas was fifty-five cents. If I had chosen to spend on dates all of the five dollars Uncle Frank gave me, then this would have been enough for nine nights out on the town with a nickel left over to spend on something else. So I will always have only the fondest memories of Uncle Frank and his five-dollar bills.

Although I had eight sets of real aunts and uncles, they

were not the only ones I called aunt and uncle. It was common practice among Czechs for children to refer to our relatives the same way our parents did. Thus, if Mama or Papa had an Aunt Tracy or Uncle Joe, we kids also called them Aunt Tracy or Uncle Joe. Mama and Papa never called their brothers or sisters by their given names in their regular conversations. If they were their brother Joe or sister Tracy, they referred to them as Uncle Joe and Aunt Tracy. This was different from the way our American neighbors did it.

I had twenty-eight first cousins (males, *bratranci*; females, *sestřenici*) and a whole bunch of second and third cousins. We kids also addressed all of Mama's and Papa's cousins by this specific term coupled with their first names, like Cousin Joe or Cousin Mary. So I had lots of cousins of different degrees.

An incident that took place when I was about eight or nine years old involving my cousin from Houston and me stands out in my memory. She and her family were spending a few days of their vacation with us one spring when Papa sent me to our pasture to check on a cow that was about ready to have a calf. My cousin and I were good friends, and it was only natural that she wanted to walk to our pasture with me. When we got there, I noticed that there was a strange bull among our cows. My cousin was afraid of cattle in general and stayed outside our fence when I decided to show her that there was nothing to be afraid of. Whether I was really trying to show her how brave I was or demonstrate my mastery over livestock I am not sure. But I picked up a stick and approached the bull, hoping that he would turn tail and run. But he was not to be intimidated. Instead, he stood his ground, lowered and shook his head and horns at me menacingly, while letting out a low-pitched bellow and pawing the ground with his front feet. Any feelings of bravery I had left me, and I turned and ran and scooted under the lowest strand of barbed-wire fence to safety. But in so doing, I caught the seat of my britches on one of the barbs and ripped a hole about four inches long. While the barbed wire did not penetrate my backside skin, the whole thing caused me a great deal of embarrassment. Not only had I turned into a coward in front of my cousin, but the rip was such that my underwear clearly could be seen from my backside. My cousin was nice about it and did not mention it while we walked back home, although both of our minds were on the incident. She even had enough presence of mind to walk a step or two ahead of me so I would not be even more embarrassed about her seeing my underwear.

On the way home, we ran into a couple of neighbor's kids. Both my cousin and I tried to act as if nothing had happened. When we parted ways, I walked sort of sideways for about forty or fifty yards, hoping they wouldn't look back and get a glimpse of my torn britches and exposed underwear.

I still don't know how my brother Johnnie found out about it, because neither my cousin nor I said anything. But for the next few days when our paths crossed while doing chores, he taunted me with, "Well, here's Robert, the great bullfighter!" But I have to give him credit for one thing. He never said anything about it to any of our family members or his friends, and in a couple of weeks the whole incident was forgotten.

One spring when my sister and I were about ten and eight years old, respectively, and there was a lull in fieldwork, one of my first cousins and her husband asked us if we would not like to go back to the Houston area with them. Of course, they had cleared it with Mama and Papa first before asking us, because my cousin would not have put them in the position of saying no to us. Mama and Papa approved, and we gladly accepted their invitation for a whole week's vacation from our farm chores. This was the only real vacation my sister and I had before we grew up and left home.

Our cousin had a Model A Ford roadster with a rumble seat, and I vividly remember the ride to Houston. My sister and I felt like a million dollars sitting in the rumble seat with the wind in our faces as we got up to speeds of forty miles per hour. That was really speeding. My cousin liked to coast down the hills in Washington County by cutting off the switch and putting his foot on the clutch. When we approached the bottom of the hill and got ready to ascend the next one, he cut the switch back on and took his foot off the clutch, thus starting the motor without stepping on the starter. This was something to tell my friends about, since we did not have hills in our county and could not travel nearly as fast because we didn't have paved roads.

My sister and I spent each night with a different relative and were treated royally. One of my uncles worked at Hermann Park, in Houston, where they had big schooners of root beer and triple-dip ice-cream cones for a nickel. To have both in one morning or afternoon was really living! We visited the zoo at the park where my uncle worked. While it was no special treat for our cousins, who had been there many times, it was really something for us two country kids. We sent colored picture postcards, which cost a half a cent each, of different scenes in Houston to our friends back home. It was unusual for children from my home community to visit in a big city like Houston without their parents. With an additional expenditure of one cent for a stamp to go on the post card, we became the envy of our friends for being able to stay in a big city like Houston for a whole week.

Another uncle and aunt and cousins took us home in their car after our Houston visit, since it was their vacation time and they were going to visit us. It took us about six hours to make the one-hundred-mile trip, partly because the roads had lots of curves in those days and also because my uncle drove at a very slow pace. About the only argument my cousins and my sister and I got into on the whole trip was which two of the four of us would get to sit on the ends in the back seat. My Aunt Vlasta settled it by figuring up the approximate total mileage and dividing it in half. When we got to the Brazos River near Hempstead, my uncle stopped the car right in the middle of the bridge. The two of us who had been sitting in the middle shifted over to occupy the outside positions for the rest of

Young Snook adults stop on the roadside for a rest and a snack while on a trip in their Overland, about 1920. (Photograph courtesy Bill Elsik)

the trip home, and the two who had been on the outside sat in the middle.

One thing still stands out in my mind about that trip, and that is how good the ham sandwiches tasted my aunt had made. It was the first store-bought ham I had ever tasted between two slices of store-bought bread, and I ate more than my share. While my sister and I enjoyed the week with our relatives in the big city, it really felt good to get back home again and to be with my family and my local friends.

All of my family members had lots of friends (*přítele*), so it wasn't unusual to have an extra person or two around the house. We got along very well with our siblings' friends. To what degree this was true because all of them were Czechs I am not sure, but it probably was a factor of at least some importance.

There was not anybody in my community I regarded as an enemy, and that included the non-Czechs. But I suppose it was only natural that there were a few who were my best

The Fojt home in the foreground and the Ptacek home in the background in the Snook business section, about 1925. (Photograph courtesy John Fojt)

friends. These were the two sons of the local ginner and one of the storekeeper's sons. We spent lots of time together either playing games or just talking about something in which we had a mutual interest. As eight- and nine-year-olds, our favorite games were hide-and-seek, marbles, mumble peg, andy over, and, especially if some other youngsters were along, crack-the-whip. As we became older, our interests shifted more to games of physical skill, such as baseball, softball, basketball, and football.

When I was a youngster about eleven to fifteen years of age, it was popular for us to have nicknames. But they were used only among closest friends. Mine was "Possum," and my brother's was "Tramp." My best friend was "Einstein," probably because he was so smart. Others were "Skunk," "Mouse," "Mule," and "Rooster." Two of my friends had Czech nicknames. These were "Krocán" ("Crane") and "Kocůr" ("Tomcat"). We sometimes called Rooster "Kohůt," which was the Czech equivalent.

I thought my closest friend was the smartest human being I had ever known. He proved it later when he became a physicist and worked on and tested missiles in the California deserts in World War II. He was intrigued by things he saw in *Popular Mechanics* and other magazines of this sort and was always trying to invent some kind of mechanical gadget. Even though I couldn't come close to matching his brainpower, we hit it off real well and participated in several things together, being natural suckers for different kinds of magazine advertisements.

Among the things that seemed to have a strong attraction for us were gimmicks promising we could win valuable prizes if we sold a certain amount of a particular product. We sold salve, liniment, and flower seeds to our parents, teachers, and others in the community, hoping to win big prizes (the more we sold, supposedly the bigger the prize). In each packet of supplies to be sold were materials describing the curative powers of the salve and liniment or the beautiful flowers to be enjoyed

Two of the author's male playmates and their older female friend pose in front of Fojt's store, on the main street of the Snook business section, about 1922. (Photograph courtesy Frank Fojt, Jr.)

by planting the seeds. Invariably neither the product nor the prizes turned out to be as good as the advertisers' claims. Our sales fell short of expectations, and we ended up by digging in our own pockets to buy the unsold items to claim our prizes. But we had lots of fun planning sales strategies and learned a lot from the whole process.

We were intrigued by new things we read about in magazines. We ordered a green powdery substance to be mixed with water, advertised as promoting a healthier scalp and head of hair while permitting it to be shaped and slicked down like Rudolph Valentino's. The slimy green concoction was similar to runny Jello before it reached its more solid form. Our hair really slicked down, but once it was touched or blown out of its perfect shape by a breeze, individual hairs stuck out in all directions, similar to Dagwood Bumstead's, but worse. The trouble was that the only way to get it slicked down again was to apply more of the concoction and recomb it. But it wasn't feasible to take some of it along with me, since my supply was in an open quart jar that sat on an apple box in our boys' room at home. There were many times later in life that I wondered if the hair stuff we used as kids might not have played a part in my being bald-headed. But I have concluded that it probably did not, since my friend still has a fairly full head of hair, and he used just as much of the green mixture as I did.

Another thing we ordered through a magazine advertisement was a powdery substance to be mixed with water to make our own root beer. After a fermenting period in one of Mama's big pottery crocks, we bottled and capped the liquid, which was supposed to produce the best-tasting root beer known to man. Papa was good enough to lend us empty beer bottles, his bottle capper, and the space to keep it in our smokehouse. While we bragged so much about how good our own private root beer was that some of the other kids also ordered it, it really was not as good as the advertisement made it out to be. Thinking that maybe we did not follow the directions just right, we ordered a second batch. But the second time around ended our root beer–making experience, because it was worse than the first one. But perhaps I had been spoiled by tasting the root beer that was dispensed from big kegs at stands in Houston the summer my sister and I visited there. It was served in a big quart-sized, frosted schooner and for just a nickel.

Although I had lots of friends, cousins, and aunts and uncles, we had only two close neighbors (*sousedi*). The closest family lived about a fourth of a mile from our house and the next closest about a half a mile. All of the other homes in our community were at least a mile from our house but a great deal farther if we did not walk. For example, three of the boys who played in our orchestra lived about a mile from us. But if I rode a mule or perhaps in a car, then it was more than three miles. All of the properties between theirs and ours were fenced in completely with no gaps or gates, the public road wound around a great deal, and they had a lane leading to their house that was at least three-fourths of a mile from the public road. Since none of us had phones or any means of checking to find out if our friends were at home, I seldom went to a neighbor's house unless I was certain he was there. Of course, chances were good he would be at home because it was unusual to just pick up and go somewhere on the spur of the moment, as people do today.

Both of our closest neighbors spoke mostly Czech both at home and in public. While their children about my age spoke some English when they started school, it was broken English. As they progressed through school, their English improved, but their Czech background was still reflected in their speech and pronunciations even when they were in the tenth and eleventh grades.

Our relations with our neighbors were very good, probably because we had a lot of things in common. I do not remember Mama and Papa ever having a disagreement about anything with any of our neighbors. If a mule or a cow broke out of its lot or pasture and got on a neighbor's property, it made little difference, because we realized the same thing could happen to anyone. We traded sausage, liver sausage, and pieces of pork when one of us killed a hog. If one of the families killed a beef for the Beef Club, both neighbors were on hand to help. If one of us broke a piece of farm equipment and needed to borrow something from a neighbor until it got repaired, we knew it would be no problem. It was not at all unusual for Mama to send me to a neighbor to borrow something needed for cooking. There never was any question about their providing it, since they knew that it would be paid back in full measure and more.

We were better friends with the family that lived the half-mile from our house than with the family that lived only a quarter-mile. Papa's and Mr. Frank's personalities fitted together extremely well, even though Mr. Frank was a Catholic and Catholics in our community, which was dominated by Brethren, were sort of looked down upon. Papa and Mr. Frank were good fishing buddies, played *taroky*, drank beer, and owned pieces of farm equipment together. When they went fishing overnight, Mr. Frank's wife stayed at our house with Mama.

All of our neighbors were good to me. I don't remember anything that came up in all the years that we were neighbors that was unpleasant in any way. All of their children who were about my age were girls. Even though our conversations were friendly when we met on the road or as I walked by their houses, we really didn't have a lot to do with each other. I knew them as good, nice girls.

Just as I was lucky in the choice of a mate, I have been uniquely blessed throughout my lifetime. I have always heard the expression: "luck of the Irish," but I never heard anybody say anything about "luck of the Czechs." Instead, philosophical discussions I have gotten involved in about how good life has been to me invariably end up with the suggestion that it was not a matter of luck but rather that I was taught the right kinds of values — to have respect for others, to be honest, and to work hard. While these things sound good, I feel this is too simple an explanation. Added to this should be another ingredient. I felt very secure as a youngster growing up in my Czech community, knowing that my family, relatives, friends, and everybody in it felt kindly toward me and wished for good things to happen to me. I give a lot of credit for my "good luck" in life to the fact that I grew up in this type of environment. When I think about my fellow Czech youngsters and their lives' accomplishments, I am convinced that we have been more successful than the American kids we went to school with. And I attribute this difference to the way we were taught and did things in our rural Czech community.

7.

Community Schools

When I started school in the first grade, the proverbial little red schoolhouse was represented in rural Texas by whitewashed one-room buildings. I attended three different schools in the 1920s and 1930s, going from a one-room to a three-room school and finally to a full-fledged high school with lots of rooms and all eleven grades in one building.

The reason for changing from a one-room to a three-room school was that we moved to another place within the community when I was eight years old. Since my second school had only nine grades, I had to leave home to live in the county seat town to complete the tenth and eleventh grades and get a high school diploma.

We moved not once, but twice in the 1920s. The first time we moved about four miles from the edge of the Snook community to near its geographic center. Papa selected the new place because he thought the land was better for farming. It had a house on it, and we could rent the additional acreage.

In those days there were no moving vans, with packing quilts and boxes, that I know of. Even if there had been, it was standard procedure for people in our community to move themselves. Since we didn't have a great deal of furniture, it did not take a lot of fine planning. As soon as the new place was available, we first took all of the farm equipment that was not being used at the time, carefully placing it so that it would not be in the way. The workstock was next, along with the animals that were needed or useful in some way; we left most of the cattle in the pasture that we owned.

Moving was harder on Mama than anyone else. The house to which we were moving could have stood a thorough cleaning, but there was not time for it. Food could not be cooked, and no hot water was to be had until the cookstove was set up. And we were not in the habit of eating cold food at our house. So it meant dismantling the stove and pipes right after breakfast and setting them up again as soon as we got to the new location. Whether Mama liked it or not, the stove had to be placed where the hole in the outer wall for the stovepipes fit the best, and that was not necessarily where she would have preferred it to be located.

Right after an extra-early breakfast, our neighbors arrived with their wagons to help us move. At first, Mama and Papa tried to have things carried out of the house and loaded in some semblance of order. But after a while, they gave up and just told everybody to take everything and load it as best they could, and we would sort it out after we got there. The men were not as careful as Mama thought they ought to be, and some things got broken, which added to her trauma. But she did not get mad, realizing everybody was there to help and did the best they knew how. As the house grew more barren with each piece or armful, it began to have an empty, hollow ring. Finally, the last bit was gathered up and thrown on top of everything else on one of the wagons. Luckily, it never rained on us either time we moved, which would have been a disaster. Papa was proud of his ability to pick a day when it wasn't raining when we moved.

Once the wagons arrived at our new location, they were unloaded at the same time. While it was easy to decide where some pieces of furniture were supposed to go, there were lots of odds and ends left on the front porch a few days until we had a chance to arrange things in some fairly logical order. As each wagon was unloaded, the driver and occupants left for home since there was still plenty of time left to do at least a half a day's good work. As they departed, they got a hearty thanks from both Mama and Papa and responded that they wished we were not moving, because they were going to miss us as good neighbors.

For several years after our last move, every time Mama saw a load of household goods going by, she felt sorry for the people. It was not until after I grew up and left home that I really appreciated how Mama felt.

We stayed at the place we rented for two years and then moved again, but this time for a distance of only about a mile. Papa bought fifty acres of the best blackland he could find the same year we moved to the farm we rented. Our main crop was cotton on both places. The second year we were living on the farm we rented, the cotton on the land we owned was ready to be picked sooner than the cotton we had planted on the rented acreage. When the elderly Czech widow from whom we were renting the land found out that we had started picking cotton on our land first, she complained to Papa about it. Papa decided that if that was the way she felt about it we would move to the fifty acres we owned and rent some extra land from somebody else. And that is precisely what we did.

The second move was made a little easier by the experience gained from the previous one, and we felt better about moving to our own place. While the three houses we lived in when I was a youngster were all similar, they were different in some ways. The quality of construction was about the same. The outside walls of all three houses were 1-by-12-inch boards running vertically, with 1-by-3-inch strips placed over the cracks where the planks fit together to keep as much rain and cold air from seeping in as we could. None of the three houses we lived in were painted when we moved, and they all had a dull-gray, weatherbeaten look. One improvement in the appearance of the second and third houses was that all of the 1-by-12 boards and shiplap were sawed off evenly at the bottom. None of the attics were sealed in, and when we went upstairs, we could see the wooden shingles that covered the roof.

The fifty-acre farm to which we made our last move had a barn too small to suit Papa. So he, my brothers, and Shine built a fine-looking big barn, which Papa decided to paint red. This is the only time I can remember all of us kids and Mama ganging up on him and trying to make a case for having the house painted instead of the barn. In spite of our efforts, the barn was painted red while the house went unpainted. But in Papa's defense, it should be pointed out that this was not unusual in my community in those days, and there were far more painted barns than houses. And there really was nothing to be ashamed of in living in an unpainted house, because this was very much the normal thing.

About four years after our barn was built, Papa arranged to buy some secondhand lumber from the local SPJST lodge when the hall was enlarged and remodeled. It had been painted white, and the lumber was grooved. We pulled off the shiplap and nailed the secondhand boards on top of the old 1-by-12s with the grooves running horizontally. Since some of the boards had cracks and the nail holes were unsightly, Papa bought some white paint, and we painted the entire outside of the house white. So when I was fifteen years old, I lived in my first painted house, and Mama and Papa lived in their first painted house — twenty-eight years after they married. This particular house also had lightning rods. Although lightning-rod salesmen extolled their virtues, ours probably were not effective, because the rod on top of the house ran down one side and stopped about three feet above the ground. So our lightning rods never were grounded.

Going to school was fun when I was a youngster. I looked forward to the beginning of each new school year and felt a little saddened when it ended. Part of these feelings may have had some connection with the fact that school was a pleasant way to get out of the cotton patch — picking in the fall and chopping in the spring. To this day, I have yet to find anything I disliked as much as picking and chopping cotton.

*Papa and Mama had been married twenty-eight years and the author was
fifteen years old before they lived in their first painted house (in 1933). This
photograph was taken in 1947.*

Not all of the Czech youngsters enjoyed school as much
as I did, but I was caught up in the fun of learning new things.
Until I left my home community to finish high school in town,
Papa and Mama used to say proudly that I was at the head of
my class, and I enjoyed being looked up to as a class leader.
Even though there were kids who did better than I did in the
town school where I ended up, I enjoyed it there also. So what
few setbacks I may have encountered were minor compared
with the good times in my ten years in the public school system, and, on the whole, school was a pleasant experience.

When I started school at age six in 1925, there were no school
buses, and none of the kids in my community got to ride to
school. All of us walked. State law required that there be a
school within walking distance — not to exceed three miles — of

every child of school age. The Snook community had three schools for whites. Two of these were the one-room variety, and the other the three-room building I have mentioned.

The first school I attended had one room, with fewer than twenty-five pupils, unequally distributed in grades one through six. There was no such thing as kindergarten or preschool training for children. Some of the grades did not have a single pupil. The youngest was five years old and the oldest sixteen. All of us, along with our teacher, her desk, a standard Webster's dictionary, double-wide seats for pupils, wood-burning stove, blackboard, and a big wall calendar advertising a funeral home in Caldwell, were contained within the confines of one room. Certainly no one could have made the charge that there was wasted space.

Standing just inside one of the boundaries of the Snook community, my first school was known as Merle School. Having Americans living on one side of us and going to the same school with them had some advantages. One was that we spoke English more than the Czech families that lived near the center of the community and had only Czechs for neighbors and schoolmates. And this gave me an advantage when it came to going to the larger schools, which were all-English.

Seventeen of the pupils in my first school were Czechs, and the other five or six were of English, Irish, or Scottish descent. There were none of Italian, Mexican, German, or any other extraction, which further explains what Papa meant by the term "them Americans" when referring to non-Czechs living close to us. Although no blacks lived in the Snook community at that time, they would not have gone to the same school as whites anyway.

I learned a lot by watching kids in other grades do their reading, spelling, arithmetic, and even geography. Knowing that all of the school kids were listening was also an extra incentive for me to do well in my recitations. I dared not miss a word in spelling, or else my sister would let Mama and Papa know about it. On the other hand, trying to concentrate on

Merle School, a one-room school with six grades, in the Snook community, 1925–26 school year. The author is second from the right, first row. (Photograph courtesy Clara Orsak)

my homework while kids in the other grades were doing recitations was difficult. On balance, though, I believe the advantages of a one-room school outweighed the disadvantages.

Our house was only a quarter of a mile from the schoolhouse, so I didn't have to walk as far as the other kids, and the teacher boarded at our house. She sort of took me under her wing; I was one of her favorites, often walking home with her after school. I worshiped the ground she walked on and helped her sweep out the building, erase blackboards, and make sure there was no danger of the stove causing a fire after we closed up for the day in the wintertime. There were no janitors in those days, and the schoolhouse was never locked. But the kids were neat and careful about littering, even on the playground. We had better manners than to create a mess, and it wasn't a big job to tidy up after the kids left for the day.

I had a head start on other kids my age. My schoolteacher brother brought first-grade books home at least a year before I started, and I was encouraged to learn to read, write, spell, and do simple arithmetic problems. The teacher who boarded

with us took a special interest in me and treated me almost
as if I were one of her regular pupils in school. My family
members were willing to stop what they were doing to answer
a question or pronounce a word for me. When I started school,
I knew my ABC's, knew how to add and subtract, and could
read "Mutt and Jeff," "Maggie and Jiggs," and the "Katzenjammer
Kids" in the comics well enough to understand what was going
on. There were no preschool classes anywhere in our whole
county, and the two other kids in my grade had to start from
scratch. This being the case, and because the other Czech youngster in the first grade could hardly speak English, I was naturally
ahead of both my classmates. So about two weeks after school
started, I was promoted by the teacher to the second grade and
completed two grades in my first year.

While Texas school laws prescribed the minimum number
of days of school each year, each school board decided the
length of the actual school year on its own. In 1925, it started
about three weeks earlier than usual, because the drought had
been so bad that we were not needed in the fields. But it also
let out about a month earlier than usual, because the new crops
had been planted, and children were needed to chop cotton.

Since the school was never locked, when the pupils arrived,
they went inside and hung any extra clothes they had on a nail
on one wall, deposited their dinner buckets on the floor directly below their particular nail, and went outside to play or
just stand around and talk until the teacher called everyone
in. She did not need a bell since the playground was small and
she could see all of us. There was no need to check the roll,
because she knew at a glance who was absent. If there was
someone absent, she did not need to wonder why, because at
least two or three pupils had already supplied much more de-
tailed information than she needed to know.

Our school day was divided roughly into four periods. The
first consisted of each grade, in order, doing their reading out
loud; the second period, spelling; the third, arithmetic; and
the fourth, geography for the older kids and whatever the

teacher wanted the younger kids to do with the little time left over. Sometimes it was a spelldown involving all of the students, in which I sometimes outspelled a fourth- or fifth-grader when I was in the second grade. But this was nothing special to brag about, because some of the kids were very poor at spelling. But it brought me some extra recognition, especially from the Czech kids, who were proud of me for spelling down American kids. At other times, the teacher would read us a story, or we would practice a school play. Just before it was time for the county school superintendent to make his semiannual visit, our teacher drilled us on the things she wanted us to know so he would be impressed. The last period on Friday afternoons was always the best, because we played some kind of game our teacher had read about in a teacher's magazine.

In between the four periods were a short recess about mid-morning, an hour for dinner, and another short recess in mid-afternoon. These were the times reserved for getting a drink of water, going to the toilet, eating our dinner, and maybe having a little playing time.

We had two two-hole outhouses — one for girls and the other for boys — on opposite sides of the schoolhouse. These were properly stocked with a Sears, Roebuck or Montgomery Ward catalog some parents had donated for the cause and a bucket of ashes. The last person to use the outhouse before school let out for the day was to dump a cupful of ashes on the accumulation of waste matter. The purpose of this was to keep flies down to a minimum. Even with this precaution, however, sometimes the fly population got high. Flies seemed to get special pleasure out of stinging us on the exposed parts of our behinds. This situation, plus sometimes a pretty strong odor and at other times the bitter cold or rain leaking through a hole in the roof, played a major role in cutting down on loitering in the outhouse.

Merle School depended on rainwater caught in a cistern for drinking and other uses, if absolutely necessary. Washing one's hands either before or after eating was not considered necessary, and the complete absence of a wash basin of any kind was proof of that fact. So as not to waste water by letting the pupils get what they wanted from the spigot at the bottom of the cistern, each morning one of the older boys was assigned to fill a bucket, put the one and only dipper in it, and place the bucket on the floor near our dinner buckets. This was supposed to last all of us for an entire day. We could have as much water as we wanted during each recess period and the noon hour. But one rule was not to take just a few swallows from the dipper and pour the unused water back in the bucket. Since the bucket was near a window, the water left in the dipper was simply flipped through the open window, which had no screen. This offered my brother Johnnie an occasional opportunity to flip water on some unsuspecting schoolmate who just happened to be walking near the open window during recess. Of course, he would apologize and say he didn't mean to do it, and he was always forgiven. If it was necessary to get a drink while classes were in session, we had to hold up a hand and get the teacher's permission.

So as not to disturb everybody, our teacher worked out a system signifying what we were asking her permission for when we held up our hands. One finger meant we wanted to get a drink of water. Two fingers meant we needed to go outside to the privy for a brief moment, and three fingers signified the need to go to the privy for a longer stay. If she nodded her head, the pupil was free to do as requested. She was downright uncanny in having a feel for when someone really did not have to get up and sometimes denied the request made by a raised hand. I cannot remember a single time that anyone had a genuine accident because she declined a request to go outside to the privy.

Since 1925 was such a dry year, the cistern at our school had only a small supply of water when school started. Furthermore, it had "wiggle-tails" (mosquito larvae). To kill the wiggle-tails, kerosene was poured in the cistern, and the water then had a strong oily taste. This being the case, the teacher asked a couple of boys who lived about three-fourths of a mile from school to bring a bucket of their water every day for everyone's use. We were sort of glad our supply of cistern water had gotten so low, because that family had a hand-operated pump that drew water from underground, and it tasted much better than the cistern water. The teacher would have asked my family to supply the drinking water, but our well water was so salty no one could drink it. We were not too happy to see our first big rain that winter, because even though our school cistern overflowed, we still imagined we could taste the kerosene which had been poured into it.

The amount of time available for playing games was very limited before school and during the recess periods, and as soon as school was out, all of us had to head for home to do our chores. So the noon period was when most of the playing took place.

As soon as the teacher dismissed us for dinner, we made a quick dash for our dinner buckets, took them outside, and sat on the ground—boys in one group and girls in another— and ate what was in our buckets. For most Czech kids this meant a piece of sausage, a slice of homemade bread, and a pickle for the main course. We did not have any kind of sandwich spread, such as mayonnaise or mustard, to make it more tasty. In fact, chances are good that mayonnaise had not yet been invented. Even if it had, we never used it in our home before I was at least fifteen or sixteen years old. On Mondays, we usually had for dessert a piece of cake left over from the previous day. The rest of the school days, our dessert usually was jelly and butter between two slices of homemade bread. No one brought anything to drink, so we did not wash our food down with anything.

The American boys seldom had meat of any kind for their noon meals, and their main course usually was jelly and bread, minus butter, which they did not like too much because it had a habit of getting rancid. So not only was jelly and bread their main food but it did double duty by also being their dessert. Another difference in what we had in our dinner buckets was that the Czech boys occasionally brought a baked sweet potato or a raw turnip. Peanut butter was something we hadn't even heard of when I started school. Also, the food was just thrown in our dinner buckets without being wrapped, and there were certainly no napkins. The only fresh fruit of any kind we had was limited to a pear, plums, or a peach when they were in season on our fruit trees.

We gulped down our food so we could play different games. Our school had no playground equipment of any kind — not even a ball. It must have operated on a bare-bones budget, because the only thing supplied for the teacher's use was a dictionary. If she wanted something for the school to help her do a better job, she had to pay for it out of her own pocket. If the items were not left over from the previous year, she had to buy a water bucket and dipper, a couple of flyswatters, kerosene and matches for starting fires in the stove, and all of the paper and pencils she used. Some parents were good enough to supply the wood for the stove, so she did not have to pay for that.

In my one-room school the teacher's salary was seventy-five dollars a month. The school year varied, but usually lasted somewhere between seven and eight months. Even though some might think seventy-five dollars a month not much for a school-teacher's salary in 1925, it was better than my brother's salary in 1933. His salary was supposed to have been ninety dollars a month, but the school district ran out of money. For three months in succession, instead of getting a check that could be cashed, he got a signed note stating that the school district owed him ninety dollars, which he could collect as soon as enough money was accumulated. All wasn't lost, though. Banks in Burleson County were kind enough to take over his scrip at a 20 percent discount. Since he needed the money, he cashed his scrip and received seventy-two dollars for it instead of the ninety dollars. This being the case, at least for the short period of three months, he made less per month than teachers had in 1925.

Although sometimes a few boys and girls played together in games like "farmer in the dell," it was more usual for them to play in separate groups. The most popular games among the girls were "ring-around-the-rosy" and "drop the handkerchief." Sometimes the older boys played together, while we younger boys made up a separate group. If a game pitted boys against boys, usually it was Czechs on one side and Americans on the other.

Occasionally someone would bring to school a rubber ball and a sawed-off broom handle, which served as a bat. With these two pieces of equipment, we played a game called "work-up." It took at least nine players — seven in the field and two batters. If nine boys did not want in the game, then girls would be recruited to fill the vacant spots. As long as a batter did not make an out, he got to bat over and over again. But when he made an out, he lost his spot and had to go to the outfield, to progress through each fielding position when, seven outs later, he got to bat again. I did not like this game too much, because the older boys batted too many times before making an out, and often school started before I got to bat — particularly if I started in the outfield.

Marble shooting for keeps was very popular, especially in the spring, about the time we got to shuck our long underwear. Every boy had his own assortment of marbles, and some were real favorites. Most of us carried our marbles in our pockets, but a real shooter kept his collection in a cloth bag with a drawstring, which looked sort of like an oversized Bull Durham tobacco sack.

We had a big variety of marbles. Steelies were nothing more than ball bearings from a piece of machinery. There were some cheap-looking clay jobs, which were not much sought after. Another type was agates, made out of quartz or imitation glass, in a variety of either clear colors or mixtures of different colors. Agates were the most favored, and every boy had a favorite shooter — his pride and joy.

There were several versions of games of marbles, and a different set of rules for each version. I usually had more marbles at the end of the season than I started with, but I was not nearly as good as some, who built big marble collections. Those who lost always managed to buy twenty or twenty-five for a nickel, the number depending on whether they were agates or clay or made of some other material.

Another game we younger boys spent a lot of time playing was called "mumble peg." This was a game in which players flipped a jackknife from a variety of positions and tried to make it stick in the ground. As with marbles, each boy had his own special knife that had the perfect balance everyone was seeking.

I was not as good at "mumble peg" as some, but that did not keep me from trying my best. As in everything else, we Czech boys pulled for one of our own to be the champion while the Americans pulled for one of theirs. But we never got into fights over it, and it was more of a friendly rivalry.

When it came to fighting, I did my best to avoid this activity. I did not see anything to be gained from it, and I also knew that if I got into a fight Mama and Papa would hear about it, and I would catch it from them. I got egged on by the oldest American boy in our school into either wrestling or fighting another boy on a few occasions. But I never fought or wrestled with another Czech youngster, and the Czech kids always pulled for me.

A popular sport in my one-room school was called "crack the whip," which brought on more scratches and minor injuries than all the rest of the things we did put together. "Crack the whip" usually involved boys only, but sometimes both boys and girls. The more who played, the more dangerous and, therefore, the more fun it was.

A line of kids joined hands, and the leader started running faster and faster, with the line of kids trailing on behind. Suddenly the leader turned in a circle. The physics of the operation was such that the far end of the line had to cover more territory than the ones on the lead end. So the kids on the far end had to run faster and faster to keep up. Soon their feet were barely touching the ground. Finally a point was reached where tightly gripped handholds gave way, and the line began to disintegrate, one kid at a time. They went falling and tumbling in all directions — usually getting grass or dirt burns, and sometimes even tearing their clothes. I do not know why we played this game, other than on a daredevil impulse, but it was popular. It was a wonder that someone did not break an arm or leg. But the ones on the tail end got some compensation for their places in the line, because the next time they got to be the leaders.

It had to be awfully cold to keep all of us inside during either a recess or noon period. But occasionally it rained all day long, and on these days we left the schoolroom only to go to the outhouse. One of the interesting things I observed was that those who tended to hold up their hands most frequently to go to the outhouse in nice weather somehow or other had better control on rainy days and did not have to go at all between recesses. And even most of those who went to the outhouse during recess in good weather somehow or other managed to skip it on a rainy day.

Our teacher was good about staying in control of conduct and the noise level during recess and the noon hour when all the kids were inside our one room. She was skillful at inventing games that appealed to both boys and girls at all levels and kept us entertained.

There was one obnoxious twelve- or thirteen-year-old American boy in my one-room school who liked one of the Czech girls. Thinking it might win some points for him with her, he thought he would impress her if he demonstrated he could speak some Czech. And why not let her know that he liked her at the same time? But he made the mistake of asking the wrong person how to say, "I love you," in Czech. My brother Johnnie's quick reply, with a straight face, was, "Ukaž pupek." The unsuspecting boy practiced saying it over and over until the next recess, when we congregated near the school porch to see what was going to happen. It couldn't have gone any better if it had been rehearsed. Sure enough, the boy approached the girl and exclaimed to her, "Ukaž pupek." Her face turned red as a beet, and in total embarrassment, she turned and ran inside the schoolhouse. We all laughed, of course, and someone finally told the unsuspecting youngster that "Ukaž pupek," translated to, "I would like to see your navel." Even though he got mad at Johnnie about it, he knew he was no match physically for my athletically endowed brother, and in a few days all was apparently forgiven.

While I got a kick out of some of my schoolmates' embarrassments, I had my share of them, too. But none of them bothered me as much as what happened to me every winter before I was nine or ten years old and started wearing long pants to school. It involved my long underwear.

Although there was an official day on the calendar announcing the first day of winter, it began for us kids, boys and girls, when Mama and Papa decided it was time for us to get into our long underwear. But there was one difference. The sleeves on girls' winter underwear were shorter, ending well above the elbow, and the legs extended only down to about six inches above their knees. Ours had long sleeves that covered our wrists, and the legs extended all the way down to our high-top shoes. It was the section in between my short pants and my long black stockings that caused me most embarrassment. But there also was a problem keeping the long underwear from extending beyond the part covered by the cuffs of my shirt.

My long underwear never seemed to fit, always being a couple of sizes too big. And the longer I wore a pair (about a week was normal before I changed, at the time I took a bath), the more they stretched. So there almost always seemed to be about two or three inches of off-white underwear clearly showing between the bottom of my short pants and the top of my black stockings, which slipped lower and lower as I ran and the elastic garters failed to hold them up, as they were supposed to. And not only that, no matter how carefully I folded the underwear over in the morning and pulled my stockings over them, they hung over the tops of my high-top shoes, giving me the appearance of having at least two or three pairs of short socks at that point. But one thing about it, it was not just me; all of the boys wore long underwear and short pants and had the same problems. Even so, I felt a sort of social stigma was attached to the obvious evidence of long underwear showing at not just one but three different locations.

I wondered why boys' long stockings came in one color only (black), while girls had both white and black stockings. Fashion designers would have done boys a big favor if they had manufactured boys' pants, stockings, and shirts that matched the off-white color of our long underwear. Then my long johns wouldn't have been so clearly visible, and I would not have been so embarrassed about them.

Much has been written about the traumatic effects on children when they change schools, particularly if they are in the lower grades. But there was nothing traumatic about it for my brother, sister, and me. In fact, we were pleased when we moved and changed from the one-room Merle School to the three-room Moravia School, which was closer to the center of the Snook community. The change meant going from a situation where Czech youngsters outnumbered American kids by only a slight margin to one in which we had them far outnumbered. Of the forty-one pupils in my room at Moravia School in 1928, there were thirty-seven Czechs and only four Americans.

Just being among a lot more kids was more exciting. Whereas there had been only three of us in the third grade at Merle, now there were fourteen or fifteen in my fourth grade. I also felt more grown up being in room two (the fourth, fifth, and sixth grades), with the first through third graders relegated to room one.

Moravia School had several advantages over Merle. We each had a desk to ourselves where before we had had to double up. There were only three groups doing their reading and other

Room two (grades 4 to 6) in Moravia School in Snook, 1928–29 school year. The author is second from the right, front row. Thirty-five of the thirty-nine pupils were Czech. (Photograph courtesy Ella Orsak)

recitations, as compared with six at Merle. Consequently, more time was devoted to each group. But at the same time, not everyone got to read out loud, since there were so many pupils. So the teacher skipped around, and we did not know when we were going to be called on to read. This gave us the feeling that we had to be prepared at all times.

We now had a separate cloakroom where we could hang our extra clothes on a nail and also a place for our dinner buckets. We also had more books and even an encyclopedia and more blackboard space. The wood floors had a layer of some kind of dark, oily substance on them, and one could even walk on them barefooted without fear of getting a splinter. The walls were of rough lumber, but they were painted. The windows were much bigger, and the white walls made things much lighter, and we could see better inside Moravia School. But just as at Merle, the windows did not have any screens, and an occasional fly, wasp, or yellow jacket created temporary distractions, particularly among the girls. We boys, of course, would have been embarrassed to be caught acting bothered by any little thing like a yellow jacket, or even an occasional black-widow spider.

The teacher had a gasoline-burning lantern she could light on infrequent occasions when the clouds and sky got really dark. So our regular classroom routine was seldom interrupted because of a lack of light. At Merle School, on the other hand, when it got sort of dark, the one kerosene lamp we had just did not put out enough light for all of us to see to carry on our regular work. Another improvement was that, instead of the big funeral-home calendar hanging on the wall, we had a more permanently mounted board on which the month and date were changed manually. I especially welcomed this change, because I no longer had to think about dead people each time I checked on the month and date.

Even though we had three classrooms, a big hallway that ran down the center of the building, and a big front porch, the school had no janitor. So each teacher rotated teams of boys and girls who performed the duties assigned to janitors in larger schools. In a way this was a good scheme, because we kept the buildings and playgrounds clean, knowing that we were going to have to clean them up ourselves. I do not remember anyone ever throwing as much as a gum or candy wrapper on either the floor or playground in all of my nine years at Merle and Moravia schools. This I attribute mostly to the kind of upbringing we had in those days. Our parents made it clear we were not to do anything at school, church, or anywhere else that we would not do at home. And we were afraid not to obey their advice.

Moravia School had a couple of giant's rides, two slides, three separate seesaws, basketballs and a dirt basketball court, softballs, and bats. It offered a bigger variety of ways to use up a lot of energy and also more opportunities to get more bruises, torn clothes, and scuffed shoes. Even though we had more equipment, there also were around one hundred kids to share it with, since the recess and noon periods were at the same time for all. These were signaled by a large bell, similar to the ones found in churches, which was rung by pulling a rope. The rope was in full view of all in the hallway between all three rooms, but in all six of my years in Moravia School, not even once did someone pull the rope as a prank to signal the beginning of a break or new period. But one thing for sure, when the bell rang to signal recess, the boys made a mad dash to claim their spot on a preferred piece of playground equipment. The general rule was first come, first served.

Going from a school that depended on rainwater stored in a cistern to one with a deep well from which a hand pump produced cooler and better-tasting water was a welcome change. An ingenious local person rigged a Rube Goldberg–type setup that permitted us to have what we facetiously called water fountains. While it was not without flaws, it was a big improvement over the Merle system, where all students drank out of the same dipper and same bucket of water all day long. The challenge for the inventor was to figure out a system in which the flow of gravity allowed the kids to get a drink simply by pushing a button. This he did by mounting the pump up on a platform a few feet above the level of a one-hundred-gallon wooden barrel and then tieing a rain gutter on the mouth of the pump with some bailing wire so the water flowed downward into the barrel. Then he drilled a couple of holes near the bottom of the barrel in which two push-button faucets were placed. So two persons could get a drink at the same time, the water level in the barrel determining the pressure of the flow. Teams of four boys were responsible for pumping water into the barrel each day, which led to a very embarrassing situation for me personally.

One day when I was in either the fifth or the sixth grade, three of my friends and I had the assignment of pumping water into the barrel. It was a hot day, and the kids drank a lot of water during the first recess and also at noon. My friends and I got so involved in a game we were playing that we forgot

The drinking-water system operated by a hand pump and gravity flow at Moravia School in Snook, about 1928. (Photograph courtesy Ella Orsak)

to check on the water situation. The bell rang near the conclusion of the noon recess, calling a halt to all playing and signifying that school would begin again within three minutes. As our luck would have it, all of the kids decided they had to have a drink before going in. After the first few persons, the barrel was dry. All of a sudden we boys, who also were in line to get a drink, realized that we were in for it. The principal, who also was one of the three teachers, demanded that everyone go inside to start classes without a drink, apparently to teach us a lesson about what happens when students do not do the jobs assigned to them.

Most of the kids were mad at us, because they just knew they would die of thirst. Others, however, were not all that unhappy, because they were looking forward with considerable satisfaction to what they suspected was going to happen to the four of us. The principal checked with my teacher for the names of the duty shirkers. As soon as the pupils were properly seated in their respective rooms, we four boys were told to report to him in the hallway.

Our punishment was several licks apiece on our behinds with a rope, with us bent over in a stooped position, hands firmly holding ankles. I never saw the rope either before or after that incident, which led me to believe that he had it available only for the most serious of transgressions. But it was not the whipping itself that was all that embarrassing; it was that all of the kids in all three rooms saw us getting it through the doors that were open between each room and the hallway.

The reactions to our whippings were mixed. Some of my closest friends sympathized with me. Others were delighted that my teacher could not save me from a whipping this time and that maybe I would not be one of her favorites any more. My sister beat me home from school and gave an animated and embellished report of what happened. So I caught it again from Papa. For the next week or so my brother Johnnie kept reminding me of the incident with the greeting, "Well, here's Robert, the great water pumper." It was the only time in all of my school years that I got a C in deportment on my report card. But Papa spared me any additional punishment for the report card, either figuring that I had suffered enough indignities or because Mama had convinced him that any boy could have made the same mistake. But I got a good lesson out of the whole affair about faithfully carrying out all responsibilities assigned to me.

The barrel to which the two drinking faucets were attached had a crudely constructed wooden lid on it that kept out insects and trash but could be easily removed by hand. One time the students began to complain that the water had a foul taste. Upon inspecting the system to see what might cause the undesirable taste, the principal found a dead, bloated toad-frog in the barrel. After removing the foul-smelling frog and ordering the barrel completely drained before it was filled again, he set out to find out who had put the frog in our water. In spite of threats, including no recess for anybody if the guilty party didn't confess, the principal never did find out who did it. But most of us boys narrowed it down to two possibilities — one a Czech and the other an American boy.

The youngster who was one of the prime suspects didn't particularly like school and was in almost constant trouble with teachers and his classmates. And he brought most of his difficulties on himself by doing all kinds of things the rest of us didn't dare think about. One cold winter morning, he showed up in our room after having been thoroughly sprayed by a skunk on a hunting trip the night before. The teacher, of course, sent him home for a couple of days, which I suspect was just what he wanted her to do.

Moravia had two separate four-holer outhouses — one for boys and the other for girls — and they were a good distance apart. They were more sturdily built than the ones at the Merle School, and the outside walls were painted white. Also, instead of just being huge, perfectly round holes (probably comfortable for an extremely fat person, but so large a youngster of my size could fall through) like those at Merle, the holes at the Moravia school outhouses were different sizes and different shapes. They were more comfortable, but the basic support system was about the same — catalogs and lime instead of ashes — and there was no substantial change in odor levels.

The number of boys per outhouse was much greater at Moravia School, as was the range in ages of youngsters who used it. Given the fact that the older boys tended to go to the outhouse near the end of recess or noon period, I opted to use it as soon as recess started even at the risk of not getting to play on the equipment of my first choice.

Moravia had a full-fledged basketball team, which competed with all other schools in the county. While the two towns with high schools had some advantages over Moravia — much larger enrollments and eleven grades compared with our nine — we competed favorably against them. Most of their boys were older, and they got in more practice time on their indoor courts than we could on our weather-vulnerable dirt court. They also had suits that looked alike and played in tennis shoes. Our boys, on the other hand, played in a variety of clothes and mostly in high-top work shoes. In spite of these odds, Moravia was the county champion in basketball more than once.

Our team was made up exclusively of Czechs, and the Somerville High School team had only American boys playing for them. They always took their losses to us seriously and played extra-hard to beat what to them were dumb Bohemians. But our Bulldogs prevailed over the Yeguas (named after an Indian tribe that lived along Yegua Creek near Somerville) at least four out of five times. While we were proud of our champions anyway, the thing that put the icing on the cake was the fact that it was Czechs beating the Americans consistently. A few times we even beat Caldwell, which had a sprinkling of Czechs but mostly Americans. These accomplishments, to us, were one more way of proving that we Czechs were better than any other ethnic group in the whole county.

Moravia School also competed in track and other interscholastic-league activities. While there were divisions based

Moravia School's basketball team, 1928–29. Moravia School had only nine grades, but the all-Czech team beat Somerville and Caldwell (both full-fledged high schools whose teams had uniforms and matching sneakers) to win the Burleson County championship and compete in the district high school play-offs. (Photograph courtesy Ella Orsak)

on age, there were none based on size of the school. I won first place in spelling in my division on two occasions, and my best friend won first in solving arithmetic problems. We were awarded gold medals, and everyone was proud of us. I remember wondering if they were proud of us as individuals or because we were another example of the superiority of Czechs over Americans.

Just as in basketball, the bigger schools had several advantages over Moravia in track because of their better facilities. While they had smooth cinder tracks on which to practice, our dirt-and-grass track was in a hay meadow across the road from the school. Instead of it being laid out in oval form, ours was in a square. Also, the black soil of the meadow was very un-

Moravia School's first girls' basketball team, 1918. (Photograph courtesy Frank Fojt, Jr.)

even and had a lot of high and low places. Nevertheless, we competed favorably and won our share of medals each year at the county meet.

When I was in about the fifth or sixth grade, we had a tall, lanky, raw-boned (his nickname was "Bones") Czech ninth-grader who we were sure would be the state champion in the mile run. In spite of our hazardous track and lack of a coach who knew anything about running, it was obvious that he had the stride, speed, and stamina to be a true champion. And besides, he was a Czech.

When it came time for us to run in the county track meet that year, he lapped all of the other contestants, and some even twice. Winners of the first two places at the county meet automatically qualified for the district meet, and he placed first by a wide margin at both district and bidistrict levels. The only hurdle left before the state meet was at the regional level.

Faithfully believing that he would be first in both our region and the state, the principal let school out the day of the regional meet so anyone who could get a ride could go to cheer him on. The meet was in Brenham, which was about twenty-five miles from Snook. This was well before the days of school buses, but a lot of Snook people went to the meet in cars. Although our champion failed at this task, he had a good reason.

The meet started about 8:30 that morning, and the mile run wasn't held until about 11:00. Having eaten a light breakfast, our hero felt that he needed some nourishment about 9:30. So he had a hamburger and a Nehi strawberry soda water. It tasted so good that about 10:30 he decided to have another hamburger and soda water, thinking he could use the extra food and drink to build up his strength and stamina.

About twenty minutes after his second hamburger and soda water it was time for the race. He quickly got out in front of the pack, and it was obvious to all that he was going to come in first. But about the halfway mark, his stomach started churning from the hamburgers and soda water. Not only did he slow down, but with about a quarter of a mile to go, he was in real pain, and he dropped out of the race. And there went our chance for Moravia to have its only state champion, suffering a defeat, not necessarily to better athletes but to hamburgers and soda waters.

The one thing I missed most after completing the grades my home community had to offer and going to live in Caldwell to finish the remaining two grades for a high school diploma was coming home after school each day and enjoying a good-sized after-school snack. There was something special about those homecomings that brings back fond memories. Even though our house was not painted and our furniture was just ordinary, there was a certain warmth inside that all the paint and handsome furniture in the world could not buy. Mama was always there waiting for her brood to come home into the midst of a satisfying aroma of freshly baked bread. There was also an additional mouth-watering aroma of freshly baked molasses cookies more frequently than Mama could afford, considering her burdens of running a house in those unmodern times. Any feelings of insecurity or doubt any of us might have had during the school day naturally melted away the minute we got home.

As soon as we got home, the first thing to be done was to change from our school clothes to work clothes. This was done quickly so we could eat a snack before going out in the field to chop or pick cotton ahead of our chores. Our standard snack was homemade bread (especially good if it was still warm), cream, and some kind of jelly, molasses, or honey. We never got tired of jelly, because there were jars of peach, pear, dewberry, fig, grape, and wild and domesticated plum jellies or preserves from which to choose, all put up at home and ready for use.

While eating a snack, I enjoyed looking at the funny papers, getting at least a mild chuckle out of them. The comic strips in those days were funny, since this was before the days of the soap-opera, detective, and bad-guy types of so-called comic strips that the public is subjected to today. And they were all clean—not even a subtle hint of sex, murder, violence, or bad guys, or make-believe creatures from outer space who were out to perform evil deeds.

Papa almost never was at the house when we got home from school. We seldom asked Mama where he was, knowing that he was off somewhere doing things in his family's behalf. If there were extra chores to be done, we got his orders through Mama.

My after-school chores changed with each advance in age and as my older brothers and sisters left home. Most of these were fairly mundane, but I remember one in particular for which I had sole responsibility for about three or four years in the winter months—taking care of our chicken eggs when they were hatching in our incubator.

Before I left home, we never bought chickens, turkeys, ducks, geese, or guineas from a commercial hatchery. Papa thought it was cheaper to buy an incubator and hatch our own. Hatching was a real art in those days. This was something that could be done any time of the year and depended largely on the degree to which our flocks were being depleted and the availability of setting hens. Normally, when we were picking up eggs and approaching a nest, which was in an old apple box in the chicken coop, a regular hen would jump out and run away. But a setting hen just sat there, making menacing noises, pecking at our hands when we tried to get her to move, and absolutely refusing to leave her nest. Even if I was successful at picking her up to gather the eggs she was sitting on, she nestled right back down in her nest again, letting me know that was the way it was going to be. It was up to Mama to decide if she wanted a hen to hatch as many eggs as her body could comfortably cover.

Although it was by no means scientific, Mama had a special knack for deciding which eggs were best for hatching. I watched her on many occasions hold an egg delicately between her thumb and two fingers, put it close to her ear, and shake it. I never did figure out her system, but it must have been some type of test based on how an egg sounded and felt to her. If an egg was weeded out from consideration, it joined others to be either eaten or sent to the store to be traded. If the egg was picked out for hatching, it was marked with a pencil and pronounced to be a good one. The chosen ones were then placed in a nest under the setting hen, and we let her go ahead and do her job.

The reason for marking the eggs with a pencil was to tell them from other eggs that might have been freshly laid in a nest by another hen when the setter left it for a brief period to get some food or water. This meant that the setting hen had to be lifted from her nest bodily every day, in spite of her pecking and general protestations. After we collected the unmarked eggs, she was placed back on her nest to keep them at the magic temperature level her body created. After about three weeks, the eggs hatched out. Even if there was a turkey or guinea egg mixed in with the chicks, she proudly took care of and defended her entire brood until they were of age. At that point the mother hen turned into a layer again.

At least once each year, usually about mid-February, I had the task of taking care of the eggs hatching in our incubator. Papa was proud of our Sears, Roebuck incubator, which could handle up to ninety eggs at a time. After Mama selected the best eggs for incubation, my job was to check on and refill a kerosene lamp that kept a wick burning, giving off the needed heat for the hatching to take place. The heat level was controlled by putting the wick higher or lower, depending on the thermometer reading in the incubator. This was not too big a job, but I also had to turn each egg over individually by hand every afternoon. I was not particularly fond of having to turn them over every day, including Saturdays and Sundays, but it was a real thrill to see the first eggs crack a little after about three weeks in their incubator. Then a small hole would appear in the shell and get bigger until a beak could be seen sticking out of it. Eventually, about half of the shell would disintegrate, and out would come a damp new chick with its first peep.

All of our family members knew it was my job to see the incubation process through from beginning to end. While I might not have been cheerful about it every day of the roughly month-long period, I was always pleased with myself and the feeling that I was making a contribution not only to the welfare of the chicks but also to my family. I missed these kinds of things, along with the after-school snacks and chores and being with my family on a daily basis, when I went off to finish high school in Caldwell.

8.

School in the County Seat–Leaving Home

While I encountered no special situations I could not handle in changing from Moravia School, in Snook, to Caldwell High School, the transition was different from when I changed from Merle to Moravia School.

Caldwell was about fifteen miles from home in a straight line. But the road meandered, making the travel distance about twenty-six miles. It also was impassable for days at a time because of mud and four creeks that overflowed each time there was a heavy rain. Since there were no school buses, I had to stay in town during the school year. So at age fourteen, I left home, without being able to visit in my community for sometimes two or three weeks at a stretch. Not only that, but changing schools this time called for some major changes in life-styles.

Mama and Papa were no longer close at hand and did not have a telephone. So I was more or less on my own. My two Czech roommates from Snook and I planned our meals, cooked our food, washed dishes, made our own fire in the woodburning stove on cold days, pressed our trousers and shirts, and did other things that were considered women's work. There was not anyone around to check on how much studying we did or how we spent our time outside school hours.

One thing that made living in Caldwell less painful than it otherwise could have been was that my two roommates and I were good friends and had known each other all our lives. We had played in the dance orchestra together, and all of us were in the Caldwell High School band. Our parents had always been good friends, and as younger kids we had spent several nights together in each other's homes.

The three of us rented one large room together. It was the same room my brother and two other Snook Czech boys had lived in some four years earlier. It also was the same house in which my sister and two Snook Czech girls had rented a room downstairs. Our room was on the second floor of the old two-story house, also occupied by its owners, who were an older Czech couple with none of their children living at home. The rent was two dollars apiece per month. We three boys did all of our living, sleeping, eating, studying, and playing in the one room and even bathed and went to the bathroom in it on especially cold and rainy nights.

Fortunately, the house had electricity. We had a single light bulb hanging from the ceiling in the middle of the room, operated by pulling a piece of twine attached to the pull chain next to the light bulb. While it was not fancy, it offered more light than what we were used to at home, especially if we were in the middle of the room. The landlord provided the light bulb, which was probably 60 watts, because a 75- or 100-watt bulb would have burned more electricity and our rent included utility costs. One good thing about the light bulbs, though, was that they lasted a whole lot longer in those days than today. There were no electrical plugs, so we could not have used an appliance or a radio even if we had had one. That did not bother us, because we were not used to electrical appliances, since our parents' homes did not have electricity. Our only door opened to the upstairs hallway and could not be locked, and there were a few signs that the landlord checked out our room in our absence.

Times were hard in the two years I spent in town. Consequently, it was important to get by as cheaply as possible. Since our parents produced just about everything imaginable, we took our food from home and did our own cooking. My turn was every third week. Every Sunday afternoon when it was my turn, Mama filled two or three big boxes with edibles of different kinds—from homemade bread to meats and a variety of fresh vegetables from our garden and food canned at home. She usually threw in a cake, which lasted three hungry boys about two days. We knew it would have been better if we could have managed to stretch out a cake for five days and considered this possibility several times. But invariably there was none left by the third day. It was not so bad not having dessert for a few days, though, because we knew if it did not rain too much and we could go home for the weekend there would be ample amounts of desserts at home.

Since it was up to me to provide the food every third week, I also had to prepare it on those particular weeks. So I learned the art of planning meals and cooking for three when I was fourteen years old. This also meant becoming adept at operating the two-burner kerosene stove that sat on top of the back end of a small table, with the front part covered with cooking materials. It was the only table we had, so it also was used for eating. Needless to say, we had not taken home economics courses that would have taught us how to set a proper table. But we didn't have need for that anyway. While I never could come close to matching Mama's cooking, nothing was ever burned too much to eat, and we never had to take anything for upset stomach or diarrhea. This is not to say that we did not come close a few times. But we were growing Czech country boys who were used to eating what sometimes were not the freshest and cleanest foods.

The real challenge, however, was making the food last through Friday noon, especially since we had no icebox or refrigerator. About the only thing we bought was a gallon of fresh milk from a neighbor for five cents every week. We usually got our milk on Wednesday night so it could be used in cooking mush, oatmeal, rice, and things of this nature after the eggs and bacon were no longer as fresh as they were the first part of the week. On more than one occasion, our Friday noon meal consisted of a bowl of cornflakes or perhaps rice cooked with milk as the single item on the menu. One time all we had left were sweet potatoes fried in bacon grease. With a goodly amount of sugar sprinkled on the potatoes still glistening in grease, this made an excellent last meal for us before a good Friday-night supper cooked at home. One good thing about our football field not having lights was that the games were on Friday afternoons, and we always got home in time for supper after we played in the band that afternoon.

When it rained a lot on Fridays, we could not go home. So it was up to us to stretch our food supply long enough that Papa or someone else could bring us some, we hoped, on the following Monday or Tuesday. We usually were able to scrounge food from other country kids in our house who were able to go home over the weekend to replenish their supply. There were three other sets of country kids in our house who brought their food from home and did their cooking. Two groups of girls had rooms on the ground floor, and another group of three boys had a room upstairs across the hall from us. And all of us were Czechs, so it was not as if we were all alone among a bunch of kids with whom we had nothing in common. It was not at all unusual for those of us who lived in the same house to swap different kinds of food items or to borrow from each other. To the best of my memory, no difficulties ever arose among any of the eleven or twelve country youngsters who lived in the house in my entire two-year stay.

While Caldwell had a city water system, the house we stayed in wasn't connected to it. So we still drew our water a bucket at a time from a well in the front yard. The only difference in what we had been used to at home was that we now had to carry it upstairs and a longer distance. Just as at home, we used water sparingly.

One improvement in what we had at home was that the landlord had a regular-size porcelain bathtub. It was on the ground floor and the only item in what was referred to as the bathroom. We were free to use it any time, provided none of the other thirteen or fourteen occupants of the house was taking a bath. But we still had to get our water from the well

and heat it on our kerosene stove upstairs if we didn't want
to bathe in cold water. So we did not bathe very often, and
when we did, it was not in a tubful of water. But we did take
a spit bath, which was our slang expression for taking a wash-
cloth and washing off the necessary parts and making a pass
at the rest of our bodies.

Although the house we stayed in was in the city limits, we
weren't connected to the sewer system, and our toilet was a
regular outhouse. It was an unpainted but sturdily built three-
holer, fully equipped with catalogs and lime, and could ob-
viously accommodate up to three people at a time, provided
they were of the same sex. When it was not in use, the door
was left slightly ajar. When it was in use by someone of the
opposite sex, one simply had to wait. If we really had a serious
urge and the outhouse was unavailable, we would cough or
clear our throat loudly as a signal, and it would be vacated
as soon as possible. Just as in everything else we did, everyone
cooperated fully in the use of the outhouse, and I was never
aware of any difficulties that arose in this connection among us.

On especially cold and rainy nights, we avoided going to
the outhouse by using a chamber pot, the contents of which
were dumped on the outhouse refuse; the pot was then rinsed
out for use the next night. This was nothing unusual, since we
had been used to doing the same thing in our own homes.

There were seventy-four students in the eleventh grade in
my senior year. This contrasted dramatically with the three in
my grade in my one-room school and fewer than fifteen in Moravia School. Approximately two-thirds of my classmates were
country kids like myself, and about one-third were kids whose
homes were in the town. Although I must have seen all of the
high school kids in the hallways or in other situations, I did
not know all of my classmates and never even had as much
as a conversation with some of them. But I knew all of the
Czech kids in both the junior and senior classes. As was the
case throughout the county, Caldwell had separate schools for
whites and blacks, and we didn't compete with the black kids

in interscholastic league or any other kinds of activities. There were no students of Mexican origin in my class or any persons of the Jewish religion.

Although Czech kids made up only about one-third of our class members, we had much more political clout than this proportion justified. We stood firmly behind each other and had more than our share of class officers and in leadership positions. My best boyhood friend from Snook, who was Czech, was valedictorian of the graduating class my junior year, and a Czech girl, whose father was president of one of the town's banks, was valedictorian the year I graduated.

One thing that changed with each different school I attended was the kind of clothes I wore. At Merle, we younger boys wore short pants that ended a few inches above our knees. The older boys wore knickers, which were loose-fitting short breeches gathered in at the knee. Black cotton stockings were standard wear for all boys. These covered all parts of our legs from our high-top shoes to the short pants or knickers so that no skin was visible. Long-sleeved, light-colored shirts also were standard wear for boys of all ages, buttoned all the way up, including the collar button.

About the time I started going to Moravia School, short pants and knickers were replaced by long pants, usually khaki-colored, which looked like the work pants the adult males in our community wore. Long-sleeved shirts buttoned all the way up and high-top work shoes also were standard apparel for boys. The girls in both schools wore stockings, with no part of the skin of their legs showing between their high-top shoes and the skirts of their dresses. A couple of American boys deviated from the clothes standard by wearing overalls, but none of us Czech youngsters wore them.

While a few kids dressed about the same way as in their previous country schools, Mama and Papa outfitted me with the kinds of clothes most of the town kids in Caldwell wore to school. They bought me the kinds of pants and shirts that were called Sunday clothes in Snook, and black, low-cut shoes.

Short-sleeved shirts were not worn in those days, but it was stylish in town not to button the shirt at the neck. For a few of the bolder kids, it meant leaving the two top buttons open.

The 1930s were before the days when trousers were manufactured to hold a permanent crease, and they tended to get baggy with wear, so we ironed our pants frequently. Not owning an electric iron, we heated our irons, which had detachable handles, on a special tin plate over the kerosene burners. We judged whether an iron was hot enough by spitting on the underside and noting how strongly it sizzled. When it was ready, we put a slightly dampened thin piece of cloth on the pants to be pressed and carefully guided the iron backward and forward over it. We discovered this to be the best method of getting a crease in our pants that would last most of the day. The next time we wore the pants, they were ironed again. I do not know how Mama did it, but she washed and ironed my clothes every weekend that I was able to come home. And she did it with tub, washboard, and the same type of iron I had from home. I really could not afford to send anything to a laundry or to dry cleaners in town, and between Mama and myself, I managed to be as neatly dressed as the town kids. In fact, I was proud of the way I was dressed most of the time. My shoes were always shined, my hands and face were never dirty, and every strand of hair was neatly in place.

There was a special reason for me to be well dressed in high school. This was because I sort of fell in with some of the upper-class kids. Although I was not totally accepted by the snootiest four or five youngsters, I ran around mostly with the upper-class crowd, which was sort of unusual for a country kid. One of the reasons I managed to break the upper-class barriers was that my academic reputation had preceded me to the Caldwell School when I beat their smartest kids in the countywide spelling contests. The other reason was that I was in the band and also had become acquainted with some of the Czech kids who were in Caldwell's upper class through Czech Moravian Brethren church activities.

The two big things in my high school were football and the band. Generally speaking, the toughest boys played football, and most of the best players were country boys. In a sense, they were the school's heroes and got more than their share of glory, not only from the student body but also the county's and town's people. The band, on the other hand, was a more exclusive organization. Unlike today, when there are separate elementary, junior high, and high school bands in most towns, kids of all ages and sizes made up only one band. The one and only requirement was that a youngster have a certain minimum level of competence in playing a musical instrument. Thus it wasn't unusual for a small fourth-grader to be sitting or marching next to a six-foot senior who played the same instrument. Furthermore, where one sat and marched within a given instrument group was determined by musical ability. So it was not unusual to have a clarinet player in the fifth grade occupying a seat which indicated to knowledgeable people that he was a better musician than a tenth- or eleventh-grader, or someone at least twice the size of the fifth grader.

My two roommates from Snook and I were three of only four country kids who played in our high school band, which comprised about ninety students. While the band was too large to have been made up of upper-class kids only, it happened that just about all of the town's upper-class kids were in the band. Attending band practice the first period for one hour of each class day, practicing marching for about an hour each afternoon, and playing at football games and concerts both in and out of town meant that the band kids spent a lot of time together and offered an excellent opportunity for close acquaintance.

Although I never occupied a position higher than fourth chair among six trombone players, I got along well with all of the band members. It never was my goal to be a first-chair player; more important to me than that was to be accepted, and the behavioral practices learned in my family stood me in good stead in this regard.

The thing that stands out in my mind about my high school band days was a source of embarrassment when it happened. Our band director was an excellent teacher, and most of the students took their music very seriously. So any big mistake really stood out. One particular winter morning, it was cold outside, and the auditorium stage where we practiced was very warm. I felt lethargic and was just about to fall asleep during band practice. We were rehearsing an overture in which the sound built up to a loud crescendo with a very abrupt ending, followed by a four-count rest before the wind instruments started up again. This particular morning, the director had skill-fully cut all sound off sharply in unison, with one exception — me. After the sudden ending, one could have heard a pin drop. But not concentrating on what I was doing, I let out a very tentative, and weak, "toot" on my trombone in the midst of absolute silence. Everyone guffawed with laughter, including the director. My face must have turned the deepest shade of red possible, and I wished that I could have become invisible. While the kids and the director were very nice about it and tried not to mention it, I knew it was on their minds. Every now and then I run into somebody even today who laughingly reminds me about this incident as the funniest thing they re-member from their years in the Caldwell High School Band.

Changing schools was something like moving up a notch each time in several ways. In addition to going to a bigger school with more pupils, I moved from a whitewashed building to a painted one and finally to a two-story brick building. The lat-ter housed all grades — from first through eleventh. Instead of a bell which rang when a rope was pulled, the school in town had an electric-controlled bell that sounded more like an alarm clock, except it was much louder. We also had water fountains (but not cold water), flush toilets, and electric lights. I was pleased to have all of the improvements over what we had been used to in the Snook schools. But there were no more recess periods. Instead, we were either in class or in what was called study hall, with only the noon hour as free time. The bell signaled the beginning and end of each class period with a few minutes in between so we could get a drink of water or go to the rest room. For the first time in all of my school years, I got to change rooms after each period instead of staying in the same one all day long for five days every week.

As soon as the noon bell sounded, my roommates and I walked home for lunch. We had one hour in which to do any cooking, eat, wash and dry dishes, and then head back to school to get in at least a few minutes of conversation with friends. Schools didn't have cafeterias in the mid-1930s, much less machines that dispensed soft drinks or snacks. So most of the high school kids either went home or brought their lunches, which were eaten somewhere on the school grounds. A little store was located across the street from the front entrance of the school. The owners, "Mom" and "Pop," sold candy, gum, soft drinks, and school supplies. It was a popular place for students to buy refreshments, and Eskimo Pies were the most popular item in stock.

An Eskimo Pie was an ice-cream bar covered with chocolate and wrapped in silver-colored paper, which cost a nickel. One of the reasons for its popularity was that the ice cream came in two colors, white and pink. Probably one out of a hundred was pink, and the person who got one of those received an extra Eskimo Pie free of charge. Every time one of the kids got a pink Eskimo Pie, he was considered to be very lucky, and just about everybody in high school knew about his good luck by the end of the school day.

Although the store was a very popular place for school kids, I seldom went there. I felt it was not right to spend money on frivolous things, knowing that Mama and Papa had worked so hard to earn what little money they were able to give me. After all, they bought my clothes and provided the food that I needed, and times were hard in my junior and senior years in high school. Another reason I was cautious about spending my money on candy or Eskimo Pies was that I didn't know when bad roads might make it impossible to go home for the weekend. If this happened, we had to be prepared to buy an extra gallon of milk and possibly some canned goods to tide us over until someone was able to bring us some fresh food from home.

While being tight with our spending money on the whole, my roommates and I usually allowed ourselves one big night on the town each week. This was on Wednesday nights, when the only movie theater had a special drawing. Our spirits were always high on Wednesday afternoons, each of us hoping to be a winner. We walked about three-fourths of a mile to the downtown area, where we treated ourselves to a big, tasty hamburger with lots of meat and onion, which cost five cents. Then we walked about a block to the movie theater, registering and putting our slips in a box. For fifteen cents we took in the movies. The theater was filled to capacity every Wednesday night because of the drawing and because the person whose name was drawn had to be present to win. After the main feature, the lights were turned on while the audience buzzed with excitement. Two slips were drawn from the box. The first prize was a whopping five dollars, and the second, two dollars. While this might not seem like a big prize today, five dollars went a long way in those days. If one chose to spend the entire five dollars going to the movies, it was enough to pay for admission thirty-three times, with a nickel left over. I promised myself that if I ever won I would offer to give Mama and Papa half of it and keep the other half. But I never got the chance to find out if I would actually do this. In fact, no one I knew personally ever was lucky enough to have his name drawn. In spite of having a feeling that the drawing was rigged, it never stopped us from going to the show every Wednesday night just in case it was really on the up and up.

The one theater in Caldwell regularly showed a Czech movie one night each month. During the school year my roommates and I walked to the theater to visit with friends from different parts of the county who were there to see the movie. But when it came time for the show to start, we walked back home again.

The price of admission was twenty-five cents on Czech nights. Given our meager financial resources, forty cents was just too much to spend on movies in one week's time.

My favorite subject in high school was Czech, in which I enrolled all four semesters in Caldwell. Since those of us from Snook attended Czech school in the summers, we had an advantage over the others in our classes. I do not know that I gained a whole lot by taking it as a language, since I already knew how to speak, read, and write it. Although I learned quite a bit of pure Czech, it did not do me a lot of good since I never used it in that form. Our Czech could be described as "Tex-Czech," comparable to the conversational Tex-Mex of some South Texans.

I graduated from high school in 1935 at the age of sixteen and look back on those years with fond memories. About the only exceptions were when I made that big mistake during band practice and when I had to take a civics course from the football coach, who I felt picked on me because I did not come out for the football team. But these were minor things in comparison with the many fond memories of school in general.

At the time of graduation, I did not have the slightest idea what occupation I would like to be in or how to go about making a choice. High school counselors were not a part of the school system in those days, and at sixteen it was difficult for me to know what to do. While farming was one possibility, I really did not think I would be good at it, and all of the land in our home community was already taken up.

Most of the boys my age who had gone to work after finishing the ninth grade at Snook had moved to Houston and taken any of a variety of jobs. A few of us had gone on to finish high school. A big majority of Snook boys got milk routes with Houston's largest dairy, delivering milk door to door with horse-drawn carts. Both of my high school roommates at Caldwell went into this occupation after graduating. One of them invited me to spend a couple of days and to make his milk rounds with him to see if I might like a job like his. Czech boys from my home community had an inside track on these jobs, because they were known as honest and hard workers, so I would have been a cinch to be employed. After going with him, however, I decided it was not for me.

I stayed at home with my parents for a couple of years and helped them on the farm. It was a comfortable feeling to be at home with Mama and Papa, knowing that I was helping them. We finally had electricity and a few modern appliances. We also had a windmill and a storage tank, with water pipes running to the house and the stock trough. But we still did not have a flush toilet, and wooden stoves were our only cooking and heating sources. While I felt guilty about not being able to make up my mind about the future, neither Mama nor Papa badgered me about it. They apparently felt that when the right time came along, I would make a decision, and they were glad to have me with them, particularly since none of my siblings were any longer at home.

After staying at home for approximately two years, I still did not know for sure what I wanted to do, but college became a major goal. While Mama and Papa and my brothers and sisters thought it was a good idea, their financial situations were such that it was obvious I would have to make it on my own.

I applied for a full-time job with the food-services department at the Agricultural and Mechanical College of Texas and was lucky to be hired over lots of other applicants. Though I thought that I had little chance to be hired, my big break came when the dining-hall manager asked me the pronunciation of my last name and my nationality derivation. Once I said "Czech," I was in. I found out later that his best and most faithful employees were Czechs. So here was a case where being of Czech extraction paid off outside my community and county.

I spent one year working as a cook in Sbisa Hall, the college's only dining hall at that time, at a salary of forty-five dollars a month, plus room and board. I managed to save enough money to enter college. After buying my books and

ROTC uniforms, which were worn on a full-time basis, I had ninety dollars left over. This was enough for tuition and room-and-board costs in a cooperative house on the campus for a little over three months. In the meantime, I got a National Youth Administration part-time job as a needy student on campus in the college's grounds department. This was before power lawn mowers were used, and I spent about fifteen hours a week behind a push mower mowing grass or planting trees and working in flower beds at thirty cents an hour.

So I left home in 1937 with many fond memories of my school days in Snook and Caldwell, where my closest friends had been youngsters of Czech extraction. The Czech connection continued the year I was a cook and after that in college, where I was an active member of the Student Czech Club for all four years, before graduating in the 1940s. Most of my best college friends were Czech, and I still exchange Christmas greetings with them more than forty years later.

9.

Staunch Czech Moravian Brethren

Even though both the Czechs and the Americans who lived near my home community in the 1920s and 1930s were Protestants, there were several differences in the ways we conducted ourselves as Christians. They were Baptists, and we were Brethren, and these two were pretty far apart in the way things were done.

While most Texans are fairly well acquainted with the Baptist church, very few know anything about the Brethren. We are Protestants whose practices are closest to those of Methodists, Presbyterians, and Lutherans. But we were not just Brethren: we were Czech Moravian Brethren, which is different in some ways from Brethren in other states and regions of the nation. These differences stem from the fact that, while the Brethren originated in the provinces of Moravia and Bohemia, a number of things were changed to fit the desires and needs of the Czechs in Texas.

John (Jan) Hus (1369–1415) provided the spiritual inspiration for the founding of the Brethren church. He was a dissident Roman Catholic priest in Prague, who denounced what he called immoral corruption within the church and clergy. He was excommunicated and burned at the stake in 1415, having at that time a large following of Czechs. His death inspired his followers to live, to fight, and even to die for the principles he preached. Fierce persecution of the Hussites took place, but they persisted in their religious beliefs under very difficult circumstances. In 1457, the followers of Hus organized a church along New Testament lines under elders. This was the start of the Unity of the Brethren (Jednota Bratrská), which was nicknamed the Moravian church by English Christians in the 1730s. Thus it is a Protestant denomination which can rightly be called a pre–Lutheran Reformation church.

As early as 1848, the Czech Brethren began to immigrate to the United States, most of them coming to Texas by way of Galveston. In 1864 the first Unity of the Brethren congregation was established in Veselí, now known as Wesley, a small community on the Austin-Washington county line. Additional congregations were organized. Among these was Snook, which came into being in 1891, but was called Šebesta at that time. In 1904 the state's Czech Moravian churches were united into one synod, the Evangelical Unity of the Czech Moravian Brethren in Texas. In the 1920s and 1930s, our local congregation was called the Czech Moravian Brethren Church of Snook.

Since all but a small number of families in my community were affiliated with the Czech Moravian Brethren church (a few were Roman Catholics, and two did not belong to any religious group), it had a lot of influence in community affairs. Our church activities set the schedules for everything else. When church members held services or meetings, no other events could have been successful, so school officials and other organizations avoided having functions that might conflict with church activities. Even the dance committee of the local lodge never scheduled a Saturday-night dance when church services were to be held the following Sunday morning.

The Americans living near our community took their religion more seriously, or at least more publicly, than did we Czechs, who had a more reserved attitude about things of a religious nature. They tended to quote the Bible, while we never made reference to the Bible in conversations with others. In fact, we did not read the Bible at home, and I often thought the only reason we had one was that we had to memorize certain verses and Psalms in it before we could be confirmed. I never had an occasion to see if their Bible differed from ours in any way other than that ours was in Czech and theirs was in English. They occasionally mentioned something they had read in their Baptist newspaper, whereas we never read our *Brethren Journal* (*Bratrské Listy*) except to check on deaths of Brethren members throughout the state and the schedule of church services.

One of the biggest differences between us and the Baptists was the way they openly expressed themselves emotionally in religious services. Theirs were lively, while ours were somber. They appeared to enter into the spirit of the preacher's sermons, while we sat politely listening to our minister with no outward display of emotions. Someone in their audience might even voice an "Amen" to something the preacher said, while this never was the case in our church. If it had happened, members of our congregation would have frowned on such goings-on, and that person would have been looked upon as being sort of odd.

The preacher in the Baptist church, located in the larger Mound Prairie area near Snook in a section known as Lone Oak, sometimes called upon one of the members to lead the congregation in prayer. In our church, the minister did all of the praying for the entire congregation. Another difference was in the hymns we sang. Theirs were sort of peppy, sung with zest, and everyone seemed to enter into them as if they were enjoying the singing. Even though some of the hymns were the same, we sang ours in a slow, draggy fashion, and the congregation acted as if they really did not enjoy singing. Their preachers devoted quite a bit of energy to pointing out the wages of sin and talking about hellfire and brimstone. By comparison, our sermons were very mild, and the minister devoted most of his time to pointing out that we should believe in Jesus and God and be good people. Bible quotations and references were relatively infrequent in our minister's sermons compared with those of the Baptist preachers.

The Baptists who lived near our community believed that dancing and drinking were sinful. By contrast, we thought dancing was something to be enjoyed by people of all ages, and drinking was perfectly OK as long as a person did not overdo it. Our minister scrupulously avoided any comment about either drinking or dancing. He was fully aware that just about every family in his congregation made homemade beer. On the other hand, members of our congregation would have been embarrassed if the minister had seen them dancing or drinking.

Another difference between us and the Americans was the way we viewed a sin. If people in our congregation had knowledge of a member committing a sin, it was looked upon as a private matter between that person and God. But the Baptists seemed to take sin more personally. If a member committed a sin, they seemed to feel that it was a transgression committed not only against God but against the congregation. They were likely to pray over a person's sin, asking God's forgiveness for it. We felt it was up to the person to pray on his own behalf and not up to the congregation.

Even though our community was basically Czech Moravian Brethren, there were two Czech families in the community that didn't attend church. We called them freethinkers, since they professed no religious faith. Their position was fully accepted by fellow Czechs and explained on the grounds that they had been turned off by the persecution inflicted on their ancestors when they tried to practice their religious faith in the Old Country. As a consequence, they wanted no part of religion. Thus we didn't see them as atheists, and they were considered good people. By comparison, the Americans considered freethinkers to be atheists and sinners and looked down on them because they didn't attend or belong to any church.

The Czech Moravian Brethren believed in christening youngsters shortly after birth, while Baptists did not christen babies. At whatever time young Baptist adults desired to join the church, they made a personal profession of faith and were baptized by immersion in a local stock tank. We joined our church when we were around fifteen or sixteen years of age at confirmation ceremonies. We had to memorize and be able

Reynalda Foyt
was confirmed
Sept. 18, 1927 - by
Rev. J. H. Horak
at the age of 14

Katechismus
Česko-Bratrský

Bern
may 31, 1913

Na základě původního **vydání z roku 1608.**
stručnějším **obsahem podaný.**

V Rosenberg, **Texas, 1922.**
Nákladem "Bratrských Listů".

The title page (ABOVE) and the first two questions (RIGHT) in the Czech Moravian Brethren Church catechism used in 1933, when the author was confirmed. This version remained in use through at least the early 1950s. (Catechism courtesy Reynalda Janac)

3

Přístup.

ᵥ Co jest Pán Bůh?

Pán Bůh jest Duch nestvořený, věčný a neobsáhlý, svrchovaná moc, moudrost, dobrota, Stvořitel, Vykupitel, Posvětitel, jediný v Božství, trůj v osobách, Otec, Syn i Duch svatý; z něhož, skrze něhož a v němž jsou všecky věci.

> Jan 4, 24. Bůh duch jest, a ti, kteříž se jemu modlí, v duchu a v pravdě musejí se modliti.
>
> 1. Jan 4, 16. Bůh láska jest, a kdož v lásce přebývá v Bohu přebývá a Bůh v něm.

2. Proč té Pán Bůh stvořil?

Proto, abych jej znal, v něho cele věřil, jej ctil, i miloval a v milosti jeho zůstávaje, na věky živ byl.

> Žalm. 111, 10. Počátek moudrosti jest bázeň Hospodinova.
>
> Mat. 15, 26. Nebo co jest platno člověku, by všechen svět získal, své pak duši by uškodil?

Questions 1 and 2 and answers are translated as follows:
1. WHO IS GOD?
   God is an uncreated Spirit, eternal and unembodied, supreme power, wise, good, Creator, Savior, Blesser, one God in three persons, Father, Son, and holy Spirit; from Him, through Him, and in Him are all things.
2. WHY DID GOD CREATE YOU?
   So that I would know Him, fully believe in Him, revere Him, love Him, and be sustained in His love, in eternal life.

to repeat the answers to fifty-seven questions contained in our Brethren catechism book written in Czech and to recite a number of selected Psalms and verses from our Czech Bible. It was in this connection that I had one of my earliest disappointments in a religious experience.

When I was about fourteen years of age, our confirmation class was told that we had to memorize and recite the answers to all of the questions in our catechism book before we could be accepted as church members and that failure to know all of the answers could lead to our being refused membership.

As our teacher prepared us for confirmation ceremonies, it was obvious that not everyone had mastered some of the more lengthy, complicated answers in Czech. I wondered how they could qualify for membership under these circumstances. But the answer became obvious when the minister presided over practice for confirmation ceremonies. He first found out who knew the answers to all of the questions. Then for those who didn't, he also determined which of the simpler and shorter answers they had memorized. He then switched us around individually so we were in a sequence to be asked a question for which we knew the appropriate answer. I thought this was a form of cheating but never mentioned it to anyone. But it shook my faith not only in the minister but in some of the church's teachings. Nonetheless, everybody in my confirmation class was accepted for membership, and I have never known of anyone who ever failed. So this procedure must have been regular practice for other confirmation classes.

Confirmation ceremonies were by far the most impressive of all those practiced in our church, and a special Sunday was set aside for the occasion. The church was filled to capacity because all of the close relatives of those to be confirmed were present on this special day, and the latecomers had to stand up in the back of the church if they wanted to see the ceremony. The church was decorated in bright-colored crepe paper, and a special section in the front was reserved for families and

The 1933 confirmation class of the Snook Czech Moravian Brethren Church. The catechism, the Bible, and all church services were in Czech. The author is third from right, top row. (Photograph courtesy Betty Bravanec)

godparents of the candidates. The girls, in white dresses, and the boys, in dark suits, marched to the front of the church in pairs, faced the audience, and then were examined by the minister on the catechism questions and Bible verses. After the questioning was completed, the candidates were accepted for confirmation of their faith, and we officially became members of the church. This was an occasion of great pride for our parents and godparents and was followed by an extra-big Sunday dinner at one of their homes.

The Czech Moravian Brethren congregations were too small and the ministers too few for us to have a resident pastor. Ours was like a circuit rider, serving as many as a dozen congregations and preaching stations within a radius of 120 miles from his parsonage in Caldwell. And a lot of places he served had no hard-surface roads. So this meant that, while we were scheduled to have one Sunday service each month, it might be canceled because of bad weather or if for some other reason the minister couldn't come. While he sometimes traded off with another minister within our denomination, we canceled scheduled Sunday services if no full-fledged Czech Moravian Brethren minister was available. Lay members from our congregation or ministers from other denominations never held services in our church.

It was uncanny how quickly our members got the word when church services were canceled on very short notice. Only three or four families had telephones, and the closest neighbors for some were as much as half a mile away. And there was no radio station to listen to for the information. On the other hand, there always was some doubt about church services on Sundays when the weather was bad. They were scheduled to begin at 10:00 A.M., and the church bell rang at 8:00 on Sunday mornings when services were to be held. So around 8:00 we listened for the bell, knowing that if it did not ring there would be no church service on that particular day. When there was a strong prevailing north wind in the wintertime, most of those living on that side of the church could not hear the bell. But, somehow, everybody in our community knew the regularly scheduled church services were canceled within a very few minutes after the bell failed to ring, even in the absence of any modern communication system.

With so many churches and preaching stations to serve and with the slow travel, our minister could spend only two or three hours in our community before he had to go on to hold another service or a funeral somewhere else. This meant that usually he arrived at the church shortly before services were to begin. When they were over, he found a few minutes to greet members and chat briefly before hurrying to the home of one of the church members to eat Sunday dinner.

I was glad when he came to our house after church, knowing that we would have an even bigger selection of foods than usual. It also meant that three or four other families would be at our house for Sunday dinner. He always ate at the first table with the men and left before it was my turn to eat with the kids. It was standard procedure for the preacher to ask the blessing before the meal with the men and afterwards to give thanks. He usually left for his next destination as soon as he ate, and that was the end of anybody saying the blessing when the women or the kids ate. Also, everyone seemed to be more jovial and relaxed once the preacher was gone. It was not that our behavior really was different after he left, but there was definitely more laughter, and everybody was more relaxed.

Sometimes the minister didn't have enough time between our service and another one to eat with a family from our church. When this happened, the family with whom he was scheduled to have dinner fixed a sack lunch for him to eat while traveling to his next location. His typical sack lunch consisted of homemade bread, fried chicken, pickles, and kolaches.

Since the minister spent so little time in our community, he seldom was in a position to do any pastoral counseling. But he was very well liked, and most people considered him to be a fine person with not only some religious education but also some common sense to go along with it. I often wondered if at least a part of their appraisal of the minister's having common sense had something to do with the fact that he was smart enough not to meddle in people's affairs and also not to preach about the wages of sin or mention anything about drinking.

In spite of having church services only an average of once a month and revivals three nights each summer, the Czech Moravian Brethren church was very strong in our community. A major source of this strength was Sunday school, which was held every Sunday morning regardless of weather conditions. Even if regular church services were canceled, there would be at least ten or twelve people in attendance at Sunday school. On good-weather Sundays, well over one hundred attended regularly.

Our Sunday school was operated without benefit or guidance of clergy. While parents normally did not attend, they

COPR. & PRINTED BY PROV. LITHO. CO., U. S. A

Zlatý text: Nebo povede tě Hospodin ustavičně. Izai. 58: 11.

"Zlatý text" ("Golden text") below a colored picture on a card, the Sunday school lesson for October 1, 1937, in the Snook Czech Moravian Brethren Church. The lesson is printed on the back of the picture. The "Golden text" reads: And the Lord shall guide thee continually. Isaiah 58:11.

saw to it that all of their children did so, and it was very well organized. It was considered to be an honor to be a teacher of a Sunday school class, and especially to hold a position of prominence, such as superintendent or treasurer.

As was the case in other matters of a religious nature, my two sisters studied their Sunday school lessons during the week, but my brother and I never got that enthusiastic about it. In fact, he and I attended Sunday school mainly because we knew Mama and Papa expected it of us and also because it offered us another occasion to see our friends. We usually arrived at the church to attend Sunday school at least a half an hour before it began and stayed another half-hour after it was over. We also enjoyed annual class picnics and special programs on such occasions as Easter, Thanksgiving, Christmas, and Mother's Day. In my days as a youngster, there was no such thing as Father's Day in Snook.

Mother's Day was a big thing in our church. We always had an overflow crowd if it happened to fall on the day we had regularly scheduled services. Catholics from our community and also children who had left home returned on this special day to attend, and all of us wore our finest. If we didn't have services, then a special program was held on Sunday afternoon in the church. Everyone attending wore either a red or a white carnation. Red indicated that a person's mother was still living, and white meant that she was no longer alive. The carnations were grown by families in the community, probably just for this special occasion, since I do not remember any other use made of them.

Mothers were eulogized in sermons if church was held on that day or in a special program held on Sunday afternoons, but this was about the extent to which they got special recognition of any kind. This was well before the days of commercialization of such special occasions, and mothers did not get beautifully worded store-bought cards or personal gifts. In those days mothers did not have to be told they were appreciated in a face-to-face situation and probably would have been uncomfortable with such outward displays of affection. To be recognized at a special program or service in church was enough as far as they were concerned.

Sunday was such a special day that we started getting ready for it on Saturday. This meant getting haircuts so we would not look shaggy at church or Sunday school. For Mama and the girls it meant making noodles from scratch; getting chickens ready for next day's standard menu items, homemade chicken-noodle soup and fried chicken; and baking kolaches or pies and cakes. These chores were done, of course, in addition to their regular cooking and baking duties on weekdays. Besides taking care of his Beef Club duties on Saturday mornings, Papa made sure the car was gassed up, ran errands in connection with lining up things for fieldwork on Monday, and took care of other business matters. I shucked and shelled extra corn so it would not have to be done on Sunday. And we got our usual Saturday baths in preparation for the next day.

We were fortunate to have a unique way of taking a bath, which was much more appealing than always being the fifth in line to use the same water that my brothers and sisters used in our corrugated washtub.

One of the cotton plantations a short distance from our community had an artesian-water bathhouse at their plantation headquarters for general use by the public. The public, in this case, was defined as white persons only and did not even include Mexicans. While it was used mostly by Americans, a few of us Czech kids took an occasional bath there also.

It was well worth the two-mile bareback ride on a mule to enjoy the luxury of the bathhouse. A healthy supply of constant, free-flowing artesian water, which was hotter than lukewarm, provided a very relaxing and soothing bath in spite of the appearance of the surroundings.

The bathhouse was an unpainted wooden construction, which showed the wear of time. It had a concrete floor and a big homemade wooden tub about three feet in both depth and width and about eight feet in length—large enough for several people to use at the same time. The tub did not have a drain outlet, so the constant flow of warm water over the top made it and the concrete floor slick with a slimy-green color. But the water was of such quality that it made suds even if we used homemade lye soap.

There was no lock or latch on the bathhouse, and the only way to tell if it was occupied was if a person left something outside or from the sounds coming from within. If I suspected that somebody I knew was in it, I could merely call out to verify it. If it turned out to be so—and it was a boy—I joined him, and we bathed together without any thought about being naked. Sometimes whole families went there for a bath, and I would have to wait my turn. But if they knew someone was waiting, they were polite enough to cut their time short and give someone else a chance to get a good bath.

Although it took at least an hour to ride Emma to and from the bathhouse and to bathe, it was well worth the time. Local people expressed the opinion that taking a bath in the plantation bathhouse was every bit as good as taking a bath in the hot mineral waters at Marlin, which attracted people with arthritis and other illnesses from all over the nation. And we had access to our bathhouse free of charge. It was so enjoyable that, by the time I dried off, the soles of my feet and palms of my hands were wrinkled from having spent so much time in the hot water.

One thing that spoiled an occasional weekend was a funeral, which was most likely to be on a Saturday. Everyone in our community who could possibly do so attended funerals out of respect for the dead and their families, and if they were held on Saturday, our work habits did not have to be disrupted. Another reason Saturday was so popular was the availability of a Brethren minister. It would have been unthinkable to have a funeral without a minister of our denomination in charge.

Since there probably were only somewhere between 200 and 250 people in our community, funerals were not held very often. But they were important in that the whole community took on a saddened air the entire weekend. When a death took place, word traveled fast. All businesses closed an hour before and after a funeral, regardless of the urgency of anyone's needs. Salesmen calling on businesses had their day's schedule disrupted when they did not have advance information about a funeral. They sometimes attended the funeral also, probably hoping to impress the store owner as well as people who knew the products they handled, like Clabber Girl baking powder, Light Crust flour, or Prince Albert tobacco. If a person in the community died, any dance scheduled to be held within a week of the death was canceled.

Very few local residents died in a hospital. Almost all deaths occurred in the home, and normally people knew that it was to be expected. Our local doctor almost never recommended an operation of any kind to be performed in a hospital. Consequently, a big majority of people in our community never spent a day of their entire lives in one. The closest hospital was about twenty-five or thirty miles distant, and it was very rare for our doctor to perform an operation of any kind. Also, it was unusual for the doctor to be present when a death occurred, but he was notified as soon as possible to lay out the body. While I did not know exactly what this involved, it did not include embalming when I was a youngster.

At least up to about the early 1930s, funeral homes had no part in our funerals. One of the store owners had a separate, small rough-built structure in which he kept caskets, usually only one of each size, for the convenience of the local people. Since a majority of deaths occurred during rainy months, it would have been impossible in some instances to get a coffin from a funeral home some twenty or thirty miles away for as long as three or four days at a time, and we Czechs had higher standards than to let our dead be buried in a home-made casket.

Once the body was laid out in a casket, it remained in the parlor of the deceased person's house until it was taken to the cemetery. It was customary for someone to sit up with the corpse around the clock.

While I could not have been more than five years old when my grandfather died, I still have eerie memories connected with the occasion. Grandpaw had been in ill health and had stayed with us in our home for a few days before he died. His body remained in our parlor for a couple of days and nights before burial. We spoke in hushed tones around the house, and no one dared laugh or even smile. A candle burned in the room at all times, and Mama wore a black dress. People came and went, bringing food and words of consolation, and someone other than a member of our household stayed in the room with the body at all times. These things made a lasting impression on me.

It rained the night before Grandpaw's Saturday-morning funeral, but it took place as scheduled. One of our neighbors came in their wagon, loaded the casket on it, and took it to the cemetery. Our family followed in our wagon. There was a good crowd on hand, most of them having walked to pay their last respects to Grandpaw. The casket was carried to the place of burial and lowered into the freshly dug grave with ropes. Once the casket was lowered, the service began.

The minister gave a sermon, read a Psalm, and prayed, all in Czech. Then those in attendance sang "Rock of Ages" ("Skálo Věku") while the grave was filled with dirt. The first shovels of dirt made a dull thud sound when they fell on the casket, which brought forth loud crying from the mourners. It was customary for everyone to remain standing at the grave until the mound of dirt was about two or three feet above ground level and finished off by being smoothed with a shovel. Then the people departed for their homes, usually taking time out to stop for a few moments to visit the graves of their loved ones.

The sadness connected with a funeral lasted well after it was over, and especially through Sunday. If a wife lost her husband, she wore black clothes in public for a few months. Also, no one in the family went to a dance for at least three months, played a Victrola, or whistled or sang happy songs. Funerals ushered in very somber times — which lasted until Monday mornings, when it was time to get out in the fields again.

Recalling what funerals were like brings back memories of the doctor who lived in our community. He was a Czech and highly respected for his medical abilities. But he also had several personal quirks, which caused most of us to consider him an odd person.

His usual dress included a white shirt, which was badly in need of both washing and ironing. His baggy trousers, held up by prominent black suspenders, were a size or two too large and in need of laundering. And his black shoes were very much in need of a shine. Chewing tobacco was a regular habit, and he did not pay any attention to when or where he spit. He also wore a floppy-looking black hat.

But none of these habits were nearly as bad in the minds of local residents as his frequent use of profanity without regard to the occasion or who was present, women included. He conducted his doctoring business out of a small, unpainted wooden building in his front yard, which had about as much dignity as Papa's smokehouse. He was his own druggist and did his own mixing of medicines. A wide assortment of different sizes and colors of bottles, some labeled and others not, were scattered all around the place in complete disarray.

But in spite of his peculiarities, everyone in our community had complete faith in our doctor. And even I had to admit that he was good in spite of his regular recommendation that a good, big dose of castor oil was what we needed when Papa told him one of his children was not feeling too chipper. He also was a firm believer in an annual thorough cleaning out for everyone, to be accomplished by a sizable dose of either castor oil or black draft. We kids dreaded few things more than having to take either of these two medicines, even when we knew they were supposed to be good for us.

Sunday was a special day in my home community when I was growing up. Absolutely no fieldwork was done on Sundays, no matter how urgent it might be. If someone had worked in the field, he would have been talked about negatively. If something was needed in either of the two stores in the community on a Sunday, it had to be bought before 8:30 A.M. sharp, because they closed at that time for the rest of the day. The two garages did not open at all, and Sunday was just too late to try to buy gas or oil. It also was a day for big dinners and four or five families getting together at someone's house. We kids never missed Sunday school and church services.

Knowing that I did not have to do fieldwork made me feel especially good on Sunday mornings, and breakfasts were more enjoyable than on weekdays. We still did not eat separately even on Sundays, but we were in a more jovial mood. Even our daily standard fare of bacon, eggs, homemade bread, and jelly seemed to taste better on Sundays.

Even though we had a more leisurely breakfast on Sunday mornings than on weekdays, there was not a whole lot of time to linger at the table. My sisters had to get the dishes done and the house clean and allow some time to get ready. Like most other girls even in those days, they seemed to me to take longer to get dolled up than was necessary. It should not have taken much time, because hair styles were plain, and girls did not have nearly as much makeup to put on. Nor did they polish their nails as some young ladies do today. But when the rest of us were ready to go, they were still combing their hair or making bodily preparations of some kind.

Mama cut up the hens and had them boiling in the pot even before breakfast was over. By the time we finished eating, the pleasant aroma of a boiling mixture of fat hens, green onions, bay leaves, parsley, and peppercorns wafted through the entire house. While she cut up noodles, she noticed with satisfaction the yellow globules of chicken fat forming on the soup, knowing that the more fat, the better her family liked it. I have had guilt feelings in my advanced years for not fully appreciating the amount of work Mama did when I was a youngster. When it came to the kitchen, Sunday was a whole lot harder for her than weekdays. And in spite of not having nearly as much time to get ready for church as her daughters, she always smelled better and looked nicer than the other women her age.

As soon as breakfast was over, Papa shined his shoes and got a fresh shave. A distinguishing feature about Papa was that his Sunday shoes were always shined to perfection. And he would have been embarrassed to be seen when he needed a shave.

Papa was so proud of his straight razor and the sharp edge on it that he kept it in a special box, lined with tissue paper, on a shelf on the back porch next to his razor strap. When his sons began using safety razors, he declared that there never would be any kind of shaving device that could come close to matching his straight razor.

One afternoon when I was about ten years old, I happened to be the only person at home. I wanted to cut a piece of cardboard and got the bright idea that Papa's straight razor was the best thing with which to do the job. Not realizing the gravity of what I was about to do, I used his straight razor, thinking I could put it back in its box and nobody would be the wiser. But it did not turn out that way. I put a couple of nicks in it, which I hoped Papa would not notice. But he did. The next time I saw he was getting ready to shave, I slipped off to play behind the barn, but with fear and trepidation. In very short order, I heard him calling me in a special way that I had come to fear. As I inwardly knew would happen, Papa used his razor strap on me for the first and only time in my life. Although I cried, I was sort of glad to get the punishment, because it relieved my anxiety over guessing what the outcome would be. And at the same time, I felt I had at least partly paid for the terrible sin I had committed by fooling with Papa's razor. I never touched it from that day on.

While my brother and I didn't spend nearly as much time on bodily preparations as our sisters, we did see to it that our Sunday shoes were shined and our hair slicked down, which was the style in those days. We kept a bottle of cheap, oily brilliantine hair tonic on hand for that purpose. When our older brother was at home, he let us use his Lucky Tiger, a higher-priced hair tonic advertised in his *Esquire* magazine. When he did so, we felt especially well groomed. But most of the time a fresh Saturday bath, brilliantine, Sunday clothes, and Sunday shoes completed our preparations for Sunday school and church. We would not have been caught dead using any kind of cologne, body powder, or deodorant even if they had been invented in those days, because we thought only effeminate boys used those kinds of things. And, for sure, my brother and I considered ourselves to be real boys.

On Sunday mornings when we did not have church, only Mama stayed at home while we kids piled in our car, with Papa driving. While 9:00 was supposed to be the starting time, Sunday school never got under way before 9:15 for some reason which I cannot explain. Since we typically got there around 8:30, we were among the early arrivals and got to visit with friends for about three-quarters of an hour outside the church building.

The reasons Papa drove us to Sunday school were simple. Like other families, we had only one car, so we used it judiciously. None of us ever jumped in a car and went someplace on our own without the rest of the family members knowing about it. This would have been a waste of gasoline, since almost always somebody in our household had something to do in the general direction in which the driver was going. So Papa combined dropping his kids off with taking care of other business all in one trip. After Sunday school, he picked up those of us who were not going to a friend's house to visit and drove us home. The other reason he drove was that he considered himself to be the best and safest driver in our household. If one of us kids picked up a tip about driving a car, we never mentioned it to Papa, knowing that it would fall on deaf ears. Mama never even once attempted to drive a car at any time in her entire lifetime.

Our first car was a brand-new 1923 Model T Ford. Papa had ridden to the county-seat town with a friend to pick up the new car, and we waited anxiously for his return. About midafternoon, I heard him chugging along between ten and fifteen miles per hour well before he turned off the county road leading to our house. I happily ran to open the gate, which was about a fourth of a mile from the house, next to the main road. After Papa drove through the gate, I closed it and jumped in with him, happy at being the first family member other than Papa to ride in our new car.

Everybody at home came out to admire the car as soon as we got to the house. It was a beauty, and we were proud to be the owners. Papa had the top down. We gave it a thorough inspection, honking the horn, testing the running boards, and admiring how all four doors opened so smoothly. This was the first rubber-tired vehicle we owned, and we admired the way the tires fit on the rims attached to the wooden spokes. Little did we realize how many flats the tires were going to have. We tried the leather-upholstered seats, which we later found out could get awfully hot on hot days and also very cold on cold days. After a half an hour or so of admiring it, Papa let all of us get in while he drove our new car into the garage we built just for that purpose.

After using the Model T for ten years for everything from hauling family members, newborn calves, and an occasional bale of hay to pulling out other cars stuck in mud, and with many flats and lots of baling wire holding different parts together, Papa traded our Model T for a secondhand 1933 Model A Ford touring car. It had metal wheels, an improved horn, a gear-shift system, and wider running boards. But like the Model T, it had no windows. We tried to keep out the cold air and rain with a set of rubberized-type side curtains, with celluloid windows that cracked and broke after a few foldings, which were put in place in ten or fifteen minutes. We sometimes used the curtains in extremely cold weather. But they were of little use in rainy weather because when it rained we couldn't go anyplace anyway because of the mud. The Model T and the Model A each had as standard equipment a set of chains which fit loosely on the rear tires and were supposed to keep the wheels from spinning in the mud. But the biggest improvement of all over the Model T was a push-button self-starter. It probably saved several men in our community from having the broken hands or forearms caused by a kickback when hand-cranking a Model T. And perhaps the biggest wonder of all: we no longer had to learn to adjust the spark and the gas as in a Model T. It was automatically done all by itself. And it even had a gear shift that was not too hard to learn to operate. We were as proud of our secondhand Model A as we had been of our brand-new Model T.

On Sunday mornings when we had church services and also Sunday school, our car made only one trip. When Henry was at home, this meant that it held all seven family members. While it was a little crowded, none of us complained about it. We knew Papa's response would have been that if we were crowded he would be glad to let us out, and we could walk. Besides, we were no different from other Czech families, who sometimes had more people riding in their cars than we did.

Papa believed in being at church or having his children at Sunday school extra early, and he faulted anyone who came late. I do not know if he ever spoke to her about it, but it bothered him a great deal that my sister Ella and her husband, Ed, were almost never on time to a public function. But the rest of us heard what he thought about it on several occasions.

Since we all went in one car, Mama had to leave with us well before 8:30 so her children could attend Sunday school, even though she did not really need to be there before 10:00, when church services were supposed to begin. But she enjoyed visiting with the other ladies. Unlike the men, the women never stood outside the church to talk but went inside as soon as they arrived. During the hotter months, they sat near an open window, where they could get the benefit of the prevailing southern breeze, if there was one at all. In the wintertime, they sat near the wood stove, which was in the center of the church. One could tell how much heat the stove generated because the women would inch up closer to it when it was not putting out much heat but start ooching away from it a little bit at a time as it got progressively hotter. All of the ladies enjoyed seeing each other and visiting. About the only ones who did not participate in this women's enjoyable activity were those who were in the family way (the word "pregnant" was never used under any circumstances in those days, and one would have been frowned at for being so bold as to say it around people).

The women talked in hushed tones while Sunday school was being held so as not to interfere with the four or five classes going on in different sections of the church. We did not have separate rooms in which the classes could be held, and the church was fairly small. Each class had to be careful about getting too loud so as not to disturb the others. But their relative locations also were determined by how hot or cold it was on a given Sunday. On hot days, we had paper fans with funeral-home advertisements clearly printed on them to stir up at least a little puff of air. But on extremely cold mornings, all we could do was add an extra layer of clothes.

It always interested me that, when we had Sunday school only, Papa insisted on driving and dropping us off at church while he went somewhere else to take care of what he called business. But when we had services, he always stayed on the church grounds, talking with other men for at least an hour and a half before church began. Topics ranged all the way from farming prospects to fishing, politics, and the latest happenings in Czechoslovakia. Papa and the others on the board of elders sometimes formed a separate little group to discuss church matters. I was proud to hear Papa's name mentioned by the minister from the pulpit because he was an elder. At the same time, it was hard for me to understand how Papa could be an elder in the church when he was so free with his cursing at home or in the field. But I decided it was because he led a double life as far as cursing was concerned. He cursed only when he lost his temper or things did not go right for him, and apparently he felt he was entitled to do so around his family. But I never heard him use a curse word in public. As far as I know, his family members were the only ones who knew about his cursing habits. The only possible exceptions could have been our neighbors, who might have overheard him cursing his mules in the field in a real loud voice.

As soon as Sunday school was over, we were dismissed for an announced ten-minute break before church started. But it usually was a twenty-minute break, putting the time church started just that much later behind schedule. Our church service was notorious for never starting on time. But this was not true just in church activities; things like school plays, dances, and meetings always seemed to get started fifteen or twenty minutes after the announced scheduled time. And this was something Papa did not like, even though he could not do anything about it. But he also was very much in favor of ending things on time and did not hesitate to pull out his pocket watch and look at it in full view of others as a hint that it was time to finish up.

When it was time to start services, one of the church members pulled the rope that rang the bell, and everyone went inside. All the women sat on one side of the aisle that ran down the center, and the men sat on the other side. This seating arrangement was strictly adhered to by everyone but the smallest of children, who sat with their mothers. It finally broke down sometime in the late 1930s.

I remember the first time a local young woman sat on the males' side. She had just become engaged to a young Czech man from Temple she had met at Hus School, which was a summer two-week religious school sponsored by the Brethren Unity. Even though she knew everyone disapproved, she was probably so much in love that she just could not bear not to sit with her betrothed on the men's side. And she was even so brazen as to sit real close to him, which also was frowned on. In those days, even an engaged couple did not sit close together when they were in public. If they were the only two people in the front seat of a car, she sat as near the right-hand door as she could get and he tight against the door on the driver's side. To sit close together was just unheard of, and to do it in church, especially on the men's side, was an awful thing to do.

I could tell that even the preacher was flustered during his sermon on this particular occasion, and many negative-looking glances were directed at the young lady. But she stood her ground, and I credit her with eventually breaking the men's-side and women's-side barrier in our church. After church, on the way home, Papa let us know he did not like what had happened and declared that no daughter of his would have dared sit on the men's side, and not only that, so close to her boyfriend — as if she just could not live without him for a couple of hours. Her mother told Mama that they lectured their daughter about her shameful behavior, and no woman sat on the men's side again for some time after that.

The Unity of the Brethren didn't believe in having Communion more than three times a year, and at the very most four times. The explanation for this practice was that Communion was a very serious matter and the participants should approach it in a spirit of deep reverence. Apparently our church leaders felt that offering Communion more often would somehow dilute the seriousness of this particular ritual. At the same time, fewer Communions supposedly caused Brethren to sin less since a sinner could expect to have the slate wiped clean only three or four times a year. But I personally knew some men I suspected committed what I thought to be sins before the sun set on the very day they took Communion.

As a youngster, I thought the minister's sermon should be shortened in deference to the amount of time it took to hold Communion. But not so with our minister, who gave the congregation the full load no matter how long it took. It was natural for me to become bored, especially when he used big Czech words I did not know the meaning of, and his sermons were very similar month after month. I remember promising myself that if I became a minister the length of sermons, the occasional injection of some humor, and the use of simpler Czech words would be some of the things I would do. And I would have a new sermon every time.

At the conclusion of the sermon, special prayers were recited and special songs were sung in preparation for Communion. The first call went to men, who came up front and spilled over down and up the center aisle. The minister first gave each communicant a small piece of bread which had been baked by one of the women members. After all males had been served bread, the minister returned to the Communion table and served each communicant wine from a silver-plated chalice. As a part of our catechism training, we were instructed to take just a small sip of wine. But some of the older men either did not receive the same instructions or disregarded them, because they took a good-sized swallow, smacking their lips afterward, indicating their approval of the taste. After each communicant's turn, the minister wiped the lip of the cup with the same cloth napkin before offering it to the next person. In the meantime, the male communicants typically pulled out handkerchiefs from their hip pockets and wiped their lips. As an observer of these things, I remember thinking that if I became a minister I would try to figure out some way for everyone not to drink wine from the same cup. This probably was because I knew some of the men chewed tobacco and had colds. I would not have wanted to drink after them, feeling that their germs were being spread by the cloth used by the minister for wiping the lip of the cup.

After all the men had been served bread and wine, they returned to their seats, and then the women came forward to be served. The same procedure was followed as for the men, but there were some differences in the way men and women took Communion. Typically, the minister gave the women a smaller piece of bread, and they took a smaller sip of wine. They also did not wipe their mouths with handkerchiefs. But it was not because they would have ruined their lipstick; neither lipstick nor rouge was worn by women in my home community in the 1920s.

Church was supposed to be over at noon, but it regularly was fifteen to thirty minutes late, depending on such things as whether we had Communion and the degree to which the minister got wound up. We wasted no time leaving church, because it was past our usual noon eating time. Sometimes we went to a friend's house, along with three or four other families, to eat Sunday dinner and to spend most of the rest of the afternoon. If it was our turn to be the hosts, we left as soon as we could so Mama and the girls could get dinner ready as soon as possible.

Once dinner was ready, the men always ate at the first table. After they were through, the women ate at the second table, and we kids ate at the third table. While our parents were eating, we passed the time playing games, and by the time it was our turn to eat, we were hungry enough to eat the table. One good thing about Czech families was that there always was plenty left so we had our fill of everything on the menu.

After dinner was the time that we kids enjoyed the most. The kinds of things we did depended upon the circumstances. When our parents went to a church meeting of some kind, this widened the range of possibilities for us boys, such as riding calves in the cow lot and going swimming in a stock tank. If our parents stayed at home, we did such things as fight bumblebees in a meadow, crawfish, and play baseball or some other game.

Around three o'clock in the afternoon, all of us got to eat a traditional snack (*svačina*), consisting of pies, cakes, and ko-

laches (*koláče*), coffee for grownups, and homemade lemonade for kids. Although it tasted good, we did not enjoy it as
much as we should have, because we knew everybody would
be going home as soon as *svačina* was over. And that meant
not only doing Sunday afternoon chores but also getting ready
to work in the fields early the next morning.

Like most other country churches, ours had little money with
which to operate. But we did not need a lot, because our costs
were low. The only expenditures the congregation had to worry
about were the minister's salary, a few dollars occasionally for
repairs, and an assessment paid to the Unity to support preaching stations and to encourage the establishment of new
congregations.

The reason our operating costs were so low was that congregational members contributed in other ways. The minister's
salary was low compared with salaries in other churches, but
his family was kept well supplied with food. The parsonage
was located in the county-seat town, and it seemed that someone from our community went there almost every day when
the roads were passable. We took or sent the minister's family
fresh sausage, garden vegetables, jars of food freshly put up
at home, watermelons and mushmelons, and even fresh-baked
bread. If no one was home, we simply left the things on the
front porch, knowing that they would be there when the family returned. In those days, such things could safely be left on
people's porches without fear that they would be stolen. Also,
their neighbors kept the items in their homes until someone
returned if they expected that the minister's family would not
be home for a while. We gave our minister a gallon of honey
every time we robbed our bees, and he never failed to brag
to Papa about how good it was. I often wondered if it really
was that good or if that was just his way of making sure he
got a fresh supply the next time we robbed bees.

Repair and upkeep costs were minimal. We had no janitor,
and the church was never locked, so that any one could get

in any time they wished. In spite of its not being locked, we never had any vandalism or anything stolen. The Christian Sisters' organization saw to it that the church was cleaned and dusted. They also washed and ironed the cloths used in Communion services, and one of the members provided the fresh-baked bread which was served at Communion. One could be sure that she did her best, knowing that members of the congregation would take note of its quality.

The men did the repair work, either individually or as a group when more manpower was called for. If a new roof was needed, all of the men who could spare some time did it together. Materials needed for repairs were obtained at cost from the local blacksmith shop, whose owner was a member of the congregation and also kept lumber and shingles on hand.

Some things, like the outhouses, needed little care. They normally were used only once a week, and the refuse was automatically taken care of by varmints or a farmer's chickens that were near the church. Someone would donate an outdated catalog when the pages of the old one were depleted.

The first man to arrive at church on cold days made a fire in the stove or opened all windows on hot days. Firewood was supplied by members free of charge. The last one to leave checked on the fire or shut the windows. The job of providing wine free of charge for Communion was left to one of the church members who had a well-earned reputation for making the best wine in the community. Papa often remarked on the way home from church that he wished he could make wine as good as that served at church.

One of the differences I observed in our church and other denominations I occasionally visited was that our minister never harped on tithing or stewardship, and I wondered about this difference. I concluded that he was afraid either that such remarks would alienate some of his members (Papa being one of them) or that it would not do any good anyway. Other than the regular collections taken up during services, at least two other ways were used to raise funds.

Each year a member set aside a couple of acres of land on which church members as a whole planted, worked, and harvested a cotton crop. The land was supplied free of charge, and member families enjoyed getting together on Saturday mornings to pick and chop cotton. The work was not as tedious as when we were working on our own land, probably because we did lots of visiting and also had a feeling that we were helping the church. The ginners, who were members of our congregation, did the ginning free of charge and gave the church a better price for the cotton than they gave individuals. All of the money went into the treasury since there were no production costs to be deducted. Even the planting seed was donated by a general merchandise store that handled different kinds of seeds.

Another fund-raising activity in vogue in the 1920s and 1930s was box suppers. These not only were important for financial reasons but also served as important social functions. Box suppers were usually held after a play or some other church function held at night. Single girls in the community, ranging in age from about twelve through twenty, prepared suppers and put them in fancy decorated paper boxes for sale to the highest bidder. They knocked themselves out to prepare the best-tasting meal possible — usually homemade bread or rolls, fried chicken, pickles, an apple, and some dessert such as pie or cake. Part of their reputations was based on how good it tasted, and this was supposed to be related to how good a wife they might make. The boxes (usually shoeboxes or square ones about shoebox size) were beautifully decorated with different-colored crepe paper, sometimes with a heart, bow, or some other fancy design for the finishing touch.

Papa sometimes acted as a sort of auctioneer, but without the fancy mumbling that today's auctioneers practice. The box went to the highest bidder, who got to eat its contents with the girl who prepared it. It was to have been a secret which girl's box was being auctioned. But this was not always the case, because some girl would tell a friend how her box was decorated. The friend, in turn, described the box to a favored boy in hopes that he would buy it.

Some of the boxes went for as little as $0.50 or $0.75, which really was not a small amount in those days. But sometimes a bid of even as much as $2.00 or more was offered, to the delight of the audience, who saw this as raising more money for the church. The young lady whose box received the highest bid felt especially honored. But the highest bid was not always intended to be a compliment, because of youngsters like my brother Johnnie. On at least one occasion, he and his friends ganged up on one of the boys. They knew their friend was sweet on a particular girl and really wanted her box. So they deliberately bid it up, knowing that he had $2.50 and would probably go that high in his desire to buy it. If he had the same meal in a restaurant, it probably would have cost him no more than $0.35, but he paid $2.50 for it. Incidentally, the particular couple involved married a few years later, so the money went for a good cause.

Just as in other aspects of life, I had a few embarrassing situations in connection with church attendance. These ranged from minor incidents that were quickly forgotten to one that still stands out in my memory.

I still blame my best friend for an incident that took place when we were probably seven or eight years old. He brought a trick pocketknife to church on this particular Sunday. Five or six boys about our age sat on the front row on the men's side. Shortly after the sermon began, when he thought the minister was not looking, my friend pulled the knife out of his pocket and quickly showed us a couple of things the trick knife would do. He then passed it on to me. I became so intrigued by the knife that I could not wait until after church to see if I could do the tricks he had demonstrated. My mind strayed from the minister's sermon as I played with the knife. Each time I could not make it do what he had done, the boys in the front row snickered. After a few minutes of being distracted by our behavior, the minister stopped his sermon to state that some of the people in the congregation were not getting much out of what he had to say.

Our parents knew who the guilty parties were, and I felt that everybody in church must have known. Our behavior could not have been more perfect for the rest of the sermon, but I did not really hear what the minister was saying, because I not only was embarrassed but knew that I would catch it from Papa before the day was over. And I did catch it, but the whipping did not hurt nearly as much as his pointing out to me that my behavior was a reflection on everybody else in our family. This preyed on my mind for the next few days, and I wished I could have taken it back. But it did not last too long, because a few days later some boys committed a misdeed in school that was judged to have been much worse than not paying attention in church. Nevertheless, the church incident taught me a lesson that I have never forgotten. No matter how disinterested I might become, I perfected a habit of looking interested anyway and of never doing anything that might be a distraction for the speaker.

Another church-related incident, which is harder to forget, happened in the latter 1930s after I had left home to work for a year before enrolling in college. Even while we were living in my home community on a full-time basis, my sister and I attended Baptist revival services occasionally. And when we were in high school, we sometimes went to church with our Methodist and Presbyterian friends, and once even to a Catholic mass. But all of these experiences left me totally unprepared for what happened one Sunday night.

There was not a Brethren church in the town, so a fellow worker and I went to a Baptist church service and sat in the back row. After the sermon, the minister suddenly asked everyone in the audience who was saved to stand up and do an about-face. Neither my friend nor I had ever been confronted with this question before. He and I looked at each other, not knowing what to do. We didn't know what the term "saved" meant, but I was not going to embarrass God by claiming to be saved for the sake of appearance when I did not know for sure. Everybody in the audience, with the exception of my friend and me, did an about-face. So there they were, the entire congregation looking at us as if we were the only sinners in the church. And the minister made our embarrassment even worse by praying for us and asking God to help us see the light and be saved.

I was glad my friend and I had sat on the back row, because as soon as church was over, we left in a hurry. We never told any of our fellow workers about what happened, and to this day, I have never forgiven the minister for putting us in this embarrassing situation, even though it was at least partly my fault for not having known better. But it was so embarrassing that I promised myself that in future years, if I was unsure of something, I would just do what the rest of the congregation did, even if God thought I was a hypocrite. It made me feel a little better to know that something like this never could have happened in a Brethren church or any other church in which there were mostly Czechs.

10.

Half a Century Later

A few changes had begun to take place in the old Czech way of life in my home community before I left it in 1937. But these were relatively small in comparison with those that occurred in the 1940s and the following years.

All-weather, hard-surface roads connected Snook with the outside world for the first time in the mid-1940s, wiping out its former position of isolation. Local residents served in the armed forces in World War II and worked in defense plants in big cities. Some returned with non-Czech spouses; all who returned had been exposed to different ways of doing things. The original community boundaries more than tripled in size through school consolidation, taking in so many people that Czechs were outnumbered by others in the community they had founded. Good roads made it possible for farmers, their wives, and their children to by employed in places as far as thirty miles away, while continuing to live in Snook. Most of the farmers continued to farm but only on a part-time basis, devoting most of their work hours to their off-farm jobs. These and other changes took their toll on the old Czech way of life that existed in the 1920s and 1930s.

Most of the staunchest supporters of the Czech language and Czech ways of doing things are no longer living. The last person born in Czechoslovakia who lived in Snook died in the 1960s. Most of my friends about my age left the community to live in big cities, where their ties with Czechs were weaker. In spite of resistance to change by all of the second- and most

A view of the Snook business section in 1948. Note that the road still did not have a hard surface and the gasoline pump on the right was operated by hand even though electricity was available.

of the third-generation Snook Czechs, the old Czech way of life has lost a lot of ground since the 1930s.

Our pasture and all three places where I lived have lost their individual identities. Each separate piece of property has become incorporated into larger farming operations. Two of the four are now owned by what Papa called Americans.

Tractors, expensive mechanical equipment, and other labor-saving devices have relegated mules and one-row farming equipment to something people my age tell their grandchildren about. Mechanical cotton pickers, harvesters, and hay balers have replaced our old, outmoded pieces of farming equipment. The latter have become antique collectors' items or museum pieces. Today's harvests are handled by individual contractors, and there is little need for neighbors to cooperate in farming ventures. New automatic-transmission pickup trucks and big rubber-tired trailers have replaced wagons and beasts of burden. Tasks that used to take all seven of my family members from before sunup until after sundown to finish are now completed by one or two persons in a matter of an hour or less, and without even working up a sweat. Women and children no longer work in the field, as a general rule.

People in my home community spend more time in community and recreational activities than working in the fields. Few youngsters have had the experience of milking a cow, and daily chores such as we had when I was young have disappeared. Milk, butter, eggs, and most of the meat and vegetables people eat are purchased in supermarkets outside the community. The days of buying on credit locally and settling up at the end of the crop year are gone.

Traveling to larger towns in air-conditioned automobiles and pickup trucks as far as twenty-five or thirty miles away is an almost daily occurrence for most of today's Snook residents. Family members go their separate ways in both the daytime and the evenings, and meals seldom find all of them present at the same time. While relatives are still acknowledged, the degree of closeness and the caring for each other that used to characterize families and kinfolk have slipped considerably.

The one-room and three-room schools I attended have been abandoned, torn down, and replaced by a modern full-fledged high school system located on a paved highway in the business section of town. The current school district's boundaries have been extended far out to encompass a territroy that had at least thirteen different school districts and more than twenty separate schools when I was a youngster. While over 90 percent of the students were Czechs when I was in the third grade, they make up only about one-fifth of the Snook school's student body today. As late as 1965, when Snook won its first boys' state basketball championship, the varsity squad making the trip to the playoffs consisted of ten Czechs and one boy of German extraction. Eight state championships later, in 1984, the varsity squad had eleven blacks and two Czechs.

The Czech school sessions my cohorts and I attended each summer were dropped sometime in the 1940s, and formal instruction in the Czech language has ceased altogether.

The Brethren church has undergone considerable change, as is reflected in the fact that its official name has been shortened twice — the first time from Czech Moravian Brethren to Moravian Brethren, and then finally just to Brethren. The days when men sat on one side of the aisle and women on the other and were served Communion as two separate groups are gone. In spite of fierce resistance by Papa and others, English has completely replaced the Czech language in church services, and the hymnals, Bible, and catechism are in English. Church services are one hour long, and congregational members arrive about the time the services begin and go their separate ways as soon as they are over. Sunday dinners involving several families are a thing of the past.

Although many changes have taken place in my home community since the 1920s and 1930s, a lot of the Czech cultural heritage still remains. And it can be predicted with a great deal of confidence that the community will have a strong Czech flavor for some time to come.

In spite of being outnumbered by people of other ethnic persuasions, the business owners, bank owners, city officials, school board, and officers of different organizations in the community are almost all Czech. Students of Czech extraction still capture a lion's share of scholastic honors and offices in the school's clubs and organizations.

A conversation in Czech still can be heard here and there, especially among the older generations. Although the young people are not nearly as fluent in Czech, it is not unusual to hear them greet each other with a "jak se máš?" ("How are you?") and a reply of either "Dobře" ("Fine") or "Polmály ale fůrt" ("Slow but sure"). Teenagers exchanging these greetings typically smile at each other, reflecting their pride in still speaking at least this much Czech.

Non-Czechs who have moved into the community in the last couple of decades openly state that the main reason for moving to Snook was because it is a good, solid Czech community and a good place to bring up kids. And they have joined the Czechs in hoping that the community retains its ways of doing things.

Many non-Czechs who have moved into the community have joined the Brethren church and respect its views and Czech heritage. While the minister, who is Czech, is not fluent enough to deliver a sermon in the language, he offers Czech prayers on numerous occasions. Czech songs also are sung each time the church sponsors a community-wide singsong, and one of the Sunday school classes still is held in Czech on a regular basis.

In the last decade or so there has been a resurgence of interest in preserving the Czech heritage. How long this will last, of course, can be only a matter of speculation. But in 1987 the Snook Brethren Church's teenager confirmation class on their own initiative memorized and recited the Lord's Prayer in unison in Czech. That was the first time this had been done in more than four decades.

In spite of the many changes that have taken place since the 1920s and 1930s, Snook is still known by people throughout the state of Texas as the place that produces perennial state high school boys' basketball championships and has good Czech people, Czech kolaches, and Czech sausage. And even though half a century has gone by since I used to hear the frequent reminder "We're Czechs; they're Americans," one can still hear a statement today that is similar in meaning, but not as strongly worded or expressed. It goes something like this: "Well, you see, since they're not Czechs, they think and do things different from us sometimes."

Bibliography

Abernethy, Francis Edward, ed. *The Folklore of Texan Cultures.* Austin, Tex.: Encino Press, 1974.

Baker, T. Lindsay. *The First Polish Americans.* College Station, Tex.: Texas A&M University Press, 1979.

Burleson County Historical Society. *Astride the Old San Antonio Road: A Pictorial History of Burleson County.* Dallas: Taylor Publishing Co., 1980.

Cat Spring Agricultural Society. *The Cat Spring Story.* San Antonio, Tex.: Lone Star Printing Co., 1956.

Chervenka, Calvin C., and James W. Mendl, "The Czechs of Texas." Manuscript written for the Southwest Educational Development Laboratory, Austin, Tex., 1975.

Christian Sisters Union Study Committee. *Unity of the Brethren in Texas, 1855–1966.* Taylor, Tex.: Unity of the Brethren, 1970.

Chupik, J. F. "History of the Sebesta Family." Manuscript in possession of author.

Comenius, John A. *The Bequest of the Unity of Brethren.* Translated by Matthew Spinka. Chicago: National Union of Czechoslovak Protestants, 1940.

Elsik, William C., and Mary Lynn Elsik. *Slovak Cemetery: Burleson County, Texas.* Houston: Privately printed, 1979.

Farmers Mutual Protective Association of Texas [RVOS]. *Eightieth Anniversary.* Temple, Tex.: Privately printed, 1981.

Fousek, Marianka S. "Perfectionism of the Early Unitas Fratrum." *Church History* 30 (1961): 396–413.

Gordon, Milton M. *Assimilation in American Life.* New York: Oxford University Press, 1964.

Hegar, Joseph. "The Evangelical Unity of the Czecho-Moravian Brethren in North America." *Moravian*, April 18, 1934.

Hermann, A. H. *A History of the Czechs*. London: Allen Lane, 1975.

Hewitt, William Philip. "The Czechs in Texas: A Study of the Immigration and the Development of Czech Ethnicity, 1850–1920." Ph.D. dissertation, University of Texas at Austin, 1978.

Historical Society of the Dallas Czech Club. *Generation to Generation: Czech Customs, Foods, and Traditions Texas Style*. Dallas: Privately printed, 1980.

Hranicky, Roy. "The History of the Czech Element in Texas." Master's thesis, Texas College of Arts and Industries, 1954.

Hudson, Estelle, and Henry R. Maresh. *Czech Pioneers of the Southwest*. Dallas: South-West Press, 1934.

Institute of Texan Cultures [ITC]. *The Czech Texans*. The Texians and the Texans Series. San Antonio, Tex., 1972.

Janak, Robert. *Czech Immigration to Texas*. Beaumont, Tex.: Privately printed, 1975.

———. "The Demise of Czech in Texas." *Texas Foreign Language Association Bulletin*, December, 1975, 6–7.

Jandacek, Antonin J. *U Našincu v Texasu*. Granger, Tex.: Našinec Publishing Co., 1955.

Kleitsch, R. G. "Social Change: Ethnicity and the Religious System in a Rural Community." *American Catholic Sociological Review* 24:222–30.

Kutac, Margaret. "English Loan Words in the Czech Literary Language of Texas. Master's thesis, University of Texas at Austin, 1967.

Macha, Helen. "The Czechs in Texas from 1849 to 1900." *Věstník*, January 6, 13, 1965.

Machalek, Richard. "Intra-Organizational Conflict and Schism in an Ethnic Minority Church: The Case of the Unity of Brethren in Texas." Master's thesis, University of Texas at Austin, 1972.

Machann, Clinton, ed. *The Czechs in Texas: A Symposium*. College Station, Tex.: Texas A&M University College of Liberal Arts, 1979.

Machann, Clinton, and James W. Mendl. *Krásná Amerika: A Study of the Czechs in Texas, 1851–1939*. Austin, Tex.: Eakin Press, 1983.

Malik, Joe, Jr. "The Contributions and Life of the Czechs in Texas." In *The Czechs in Texas: A Symposium*, ed. Clinton Machann. College Station, Tex.: Texas A&M University College of Liberal Arts, 1979, pp. 11–18.

————. "Efforts to Promote the Study of the Czech Language and Culture in Texas." Master's thesis, University of Texas at Austin, 1947.

Maresh, Henry R. "The Czechs in Texas." *Southwestern Historical Quarterly* 50 (October, 1946): 236–40.

Matcek, Gabriel C., and William C. Elsik. *On the Occasion of the Frances Sebesta Mikeska Hejl Sumsal Reunion.* Houston: Privately printed, 1980.

Mendl, James. "Historical Czech and Moravian Dialects in the New World." Master's thesis, University of Texas at Austin, 1976.

Morkovsky, Alois J. "The Church and the Czechs in Texas." In *The Czechs in Texas: A Symposium,* ed. Clinton Machann. College Station, Tex.: Texas A&M University College of Liberal Arts, 1979, pp. 88–94.

Pazdral, Olga. "Czech Folklore in Texas." Master's thesis, University of Texas at Austin, 1942.

Roucek, Joseph Slabey. "The Moravian Brethren in America." *Social Studies* 43 (February, 1952): 58–61.

Schattschneider, Allen W. *Through Five Hundred Years: A Popular History of the Moravian Church.* Winston-Salem, N.C.: Comenius Press, 1956.

Skrabanek, Robert L. "Czechs in Texas." *Věstník* 72, no. 12 (1984): 10–12.

————. "Demographic Changes in a Texas Czech-American Rural Community." In *The Czechs in Texas: A Symposium,* ed. Clinton Machann. College Station, Tex.: Texas A&M University College of Liberal Arts, 1979, pp. 115–21.

————. "Forms of Cooperation and Mutual Aid in a Czech-American Rural Community." *Southwestern Social Science Quarterly* 30, no. 3 (1949): 183–87.

————. "Influence of Cultural Background on Farming Practices in a Czech-American Rural Community." *Southwestern Social Science Quarterly* 31, no. 4 (1951): 258–66.

————. "Snook: A Uniqueness in Czech Culture." In *Czech Footprints across the Bluebonnet Fields of Texas: Second Czech Symposium,* ed. Anjanette Mesecke. Austin: Czech Ex-Students Association of Texas [CESAT], 1983, pp. 58–70.

————. "Social Life in a Czech-American Rural Community." *Rural Sociology* 15, no. 3 (1950): 221–31.

————. "Social Organization and Change in a Czech-American Rural Community: A Sociological Study of Snook, Texas." Ph.D. dissertation, Louisiana State University, 1949.

————. "Working Together Makes Snook a Good Community." *Progressive Farmer* 65, no. 3 (1950): 86–87.

Skrivanek, John M. "The Education of Czechs in Texas." Master's thesis, University of Texas at Austin, 1946.

Slavonic Benevolent Order of the State of Texas [SPJST]. *Constitution and By-laws.* 1902, 1916, 1920, 1924, 1928, 1932, 1936, 1940.

Slovacek, Marvin. "A Sixty Year Insurance History of the Slavonic Benevolent Order of the State of Texas." Master's thesis, University of Texas at Austin, 1956.

Southwest Educational Development Laboratory, Austin, Texas. "Texas Heritage Unit (Czechs, Poles and Germans)." In Ethnic Heritage Studies Program, Southwest Educational Development Laboratory, 1975. Unpublished.

Stasney, Mollie Emma. "The Czechs in Texas." Master's thesis, University of Texas at Austin, 1938.

Webb, Walter Prescott et al., eds. *The Handbook of Texas.* Vol. 1. Austin: Texas State Historical Association, 1952.

Index

AAA Farm Program, 68
Agricultural and Mechanical College of Texas, 81; attending, 190–91; enrolling at, 107. *See also* Texas A&M University
"Amos 'n' Andy," 80
appliances, electrical, 179
auctions, 221–22
Aunt Mary, 135
aunts: relationships with, 135–38
Aunt Vlasta, 140
Austin County, 9
automobiles. *See* cars

baling, 42–45
band: playing in, 178–79, 184–86. *See also* orchestra
Baptists, 96, 192, 223; compared with Brethren, 194–95
barbers, 117
baseball, 105
basketball, 171–72, 229
bathhouse, 204–205
bathing, 181–82, 204
Beef Club, 77, 84–85, 146, 204; breakfast, 85–86; photograph, 86
beehives, 41. *See also* honey
beer: drinking, 97–98, 147; making, 96–99
behavior. *See* conduct
blackland, 150; value of, 25, 27
Blackland Prairie Soil Region: immigration to, 9

blackleg: cures for, 36
Bohemia, 76
"Bones" (track star): memories of, 173–74
box suppers, 221–22
Brazos River, 140; fishing in, 121
breakfast: Beef Club, 85–86; description of, 20–22
Brenham, Texas, 174
Brethren. *See* Czech Moravian Brethren
Brethren Journal, 194
Brethren Unity, 218
Brinkley, Dr. "Goat Gland," 81
Brummel, Beau, 103
Bull Durham, 125
Burleson County, 10, 159; immigration to, 9
butchering, 86–89
butter making, 95

Caldwell, Texas, 13, 14, 126, 174, 183; establishment of, 10; living in, 178–80, 189; schools in, 182–83
Caldwell High School, 113, 178
Caldwell High School Band, 186
card playing, 98, 147
cars: buying, 212; driving, 125–26, 212
catechism book, 196–97, 198
Cat Spring, Texas: immigration to, 9
cattle: caring for, 31–32, 35–36

Cemetery Association, 77
Charlie (brother-in-law), 119–20
chopping, 7–8, 47, 58–59, 66–67, 151, 155
chores: types of, 19–20, 32–33, 175–76. *See also* farm work
Christian Sisters' organization, 220
Christmas, 122–23, 191, 203
church services, 11–12, 222–24; costs of, 219–20; description of, 215–18; fund raising for, 220–22; preparing for, 209–11, 213–14
cigarettes, 125
circuit riders, 199–201
Clabber Girl, 206
clothes: funeral, 207; grandparents', 134–35; school, 183–84
college, 190–91. *See also* Agricultural and Mechanical College of Texas
Communion, 218, 220, 228; preparing for, 217; seriousness of, 216–18
conduct: at school, 162–63, 169–70. *See also* punishment
confirmation, 198–99
confirmation class, 199, 229
conversation: topics of, 79–80
cooking, 64–66, 146, 179–80; Sunday, 209–10, 218–19
cooperatives, 11, 75, 76, 77
corn: harvesting, 61–62; planting, 54–58; shucking, 62–63; uses for, 61–62
corncobs: uses for, 62
cotton, 22, 221; chopping, 58–59, 63–64, 66–67, 151, 155; ginning, 221; growing, 46, 63–64; harvesting, 52–54, 69, 71–73, 150, 151; planting, 54–57, 66–67; prices of, 26–27; samples (photo), 127. *See also* seed
cotton gin, 77; going to, 126; smoking behind, 125

cotton pickers (photographs), 53, 55, 70. *See also* hired hands
cousins: relationships with, 138–41
"crack the whip," 161–62
crops, 22, 50. *See also* corn; cotton; vegetables
Czech Moravian Brethren, 131, 184, 192, 201, 203; beliefs of, 194–95; catechism of, 196–99; changes for, 228–29; "Golden text" of, 202; holidays and, 203; immigration of, 193; ministers of, 199–201; Mother's Day and, 203–204
Czech Moravian Brethren Church: building of, 12–13, 193
"Czech Music Hour," 81
Czechoslovakian Benevolent Society, 11

Dabney Hill, Texas, 14
dance committee, 128
dances, 128–31, 178–79
dating, 119–20, 131–32
deaths: mourning, 205–208
Delco system, 111
Depression. *See* Great Depression
diet, 83–90
doctors, 208–209
dress. *See* clothes
driving, 125–26, 212
drought, 36

Easter, 203
Ed (brother-in-law), 110–11, 213
eggs: hatching, 176–77
electrical appliances, 179
electricity, 179, 186
Emma (mule), 28, 29, 30, 58, 205
entertainment, 77–83, 81–82, 124–26, 128–31, 141, 143–45, 188
Eskimo Pies, 187–88. *See also* ice cream
Esquire, 211

family: relationships, 82–83; togetherness, 77–80
Farmer's Almanac, 50
Farmers' Mutual Protective Society, 11, 77
farm work, 7–8, 17–33, 176–77;
changes in, 226–27; Czechs
and, 16–17; thoughts about,
17–18. *See also* chores
Father's Day, 203
Fayette County, 10
fishing, 117–18, 121
flush toilets, 186
fodder making, 60–61
Fojt home, 142
Fojt's general merchandise store,
15, 106, 110, 144
Fojt's gin, 15–127
food, 83–90; canning, 94–95; at
school, 158–59, 179–81; at Sunday dinner, 209–10, 218–19
football, 113–14, 185, 189
Frank, Mr.: friendship with, 146–
47
fried mountain oysters, 35
friends, 144; activities with, 141,
143–47
Frydek, Texas: dance at, 130–31
fund raising: for church, 220–22
funerals, 205–208

Galveston, Texas, 10; immigration
through, 9
games, 159, 160–62
gardens, 22–25, 46
ginning, 221. *See also* cotton gin
"Golden text," 202
graduating, 189–90
grandparents: dress of, 134–35; respect for, 133–35
Great Depression, 68
"Green Meadow Waltz," 80

haircuts, 117
hair tonic, 144–45, 211

harvesting, 52–54, 61–62, 69, 71–
73, 150, 151
hatching: art of, 176–77
hay baling, 42–45
Hempstead, Texas, 140
heritage, 8–9, 226–29
Hermann Park, 140
hired hands, 53, 55; fixing dinner
for, 64–66; opinion of, 72; pay
for, 71–72; trouble with, 67–68;
water for, 66–67, 71. *See also*
cotton pickers
home remedies, 93–94
honey: as medicine, 93; processing, 90–93. *See also* beehives;
medicine
horses, 29–30
house. *See* Skrabanek house
Houston, Texas, 136–37, 139–41
Hus, Jan, 192–93
Husbandman: reading, 50
Hus School, 216
Hussites, 192–93

ice cream, 8, 32, 72, 140. *See also*
Eskimo Pies
illness. *See* sickness
immigration, 9
incubation, 176–77
insecticides, 24

Jack (mule), 30
Jolson, Al, 104

Kate (mule), 28, 29, 30, 46; prob-
lems with, 23–24, 120
"Katzenjammer Kids," 155
King, Wayne, 129
Kocurek family, Martin, 10
KPRC (Houston), 81
Kulhanek, Frank, 73

labor. *See* farm work
land: breaking of, 46–47; payment
for, 25–26
Light Crust flour, 82, 206

lightning rods, 151
livestock: caring for, 31–32, 36–39
Lizzie (hand), 64, 85, 88
Lodge Slovan of the Slovanic Be-
nevolent Society. *See* SPJST
Lombardo, Guy, 80, 129
Lone Oak, Texas, 194
"Lone Star Ambassadors," 130
long underwear, 163–64
Lucky Strikes, 125
Lucky Tiger, 211
lunch, school, 158–59, 187
Lutherans, 192
lye soap, 95–96, 205

Mabel (mule), 30
magazines: ordering from, 144–45
"Maggie and Jiggs," 155
marbles, 160–61
Marlin, Texas: mineral waters at,
205
marriage, 76, 109–10, 120, 132, 147
Mary (mule), 28, 29, 30, 31, 58
Masarýk, Tomáš G., 68
medicine: for screwworm, 35;
types of, 93–94; use of, 208.
See also money; sickness; livestock, caring for
Merle School, 153, 164, 166, 170,
178; class photograph at, 154;
description of, 156–57
Methodists, 192, 223
middlebuster plow, 47, 48
Mikula family, Joe, 10
milking, 20, 32–33
mineral waters, 205
ministers, 199–201, 220
Model A Ford, 137, 139, 212
Model T Ford, 102, 104, 126, 212
Montgomery Ward catalog, 62,
156
Moravia, 76
Moravian Brethren. *See* Czech
Moravian Brethren
Moravia School, 114, 178, 182,
183; building, 11; description

Moravia School (*cont.*)
of, 164–67, 170–71; photographs at, 165, 172, 173; sports
at, 171–74
Mother's Day, 203–204
Mound Prairie, Texas, 12–13, 194
mourning, 205–208
movies, 72, 104, 119; cost of, 188;
Czech, 188–89
moving, 148–51
mules: caring for, 31; problems
with, 23–24, 119–20; working
with, 27–31, 58–59
music, 124–26; making, 129–31
"Mutt and Jeff," 155

National Youth Administration:
job with, 191
Nehi soda waters, 72, 126, 174
neighbors, 145–47
New Tabor, Texas, 9–10
nicknames, 143
Nový Tábor. *See* New Tabor,
Texas

O'Daniel, W. Lee ("Pappy"), 82
orchestra: playing in, 129–31, 145,
178–79. *See also* band
outhouses, 156, 170–71

parsonage, 220
pastures, 40–41
Pentecostal church, 131
phonograph, 80–81
piano recital, 124–25. *See also*
music
pickers. *See* cotton pickers
picture shows. *See* movies
Pinex, 93
planting, 54–58, 66–67
"The Polka Ambassadors," 130
Popular Mechanics, 143
post office: acquiring a, 14
potato bugs, 24–25
pranks, 108–109, 112–13, 157,
162–63

preaching stations, 200
Presbyterians, 192, 223
Prince Albert, 125, 206
produce. *See* vegetables
Prohibition, 100
Ptacek home, 142
Ptacek's general merchandise store, 100
punishment, 210–11; at school, 169–70. *See also* conduct

radio, 81–82
Raleigh Company, 94
REA. *See* Rural Electrification Administration
record player. *See* phonograph
"Red Wine Polka," 80
relatives: relationships with, 82–83, 135–41
"Rock of Ages," 207
Roman Catholics, 112, 192, 193, 223
Roosevelt, Franklin D., 68–69
root beer making, 145
Ross Prairie, Texas, 10
ROTC uniforms, 191
Rural Electrification Administration, 68
RVOS. *See* Farmers' Mutual Protective Society

Saint Jacob's Catholic Church, 12
saloon, 100
sauerkraut making, 82–83
sausage, 229; making, 87–89; trading, 89–90, 146
Sbisa Hall, 190
school, 101, 151–56; changes in, 186–87; conduct at, 162–63, 169–70; graduation from, 189–90; lunch at, 158–59, 187; punishment at, 169–70; water for, 157–58, 167, 169
schoolhouses: description of, 148
screwworms, 31, 35

Sears, Roebuck catalog, 62, 72, 156
Sears, Roebuck incubator, 177
Sebesta, Texas, 13
Sebesta's Corner, 13
seed, 54, 57; cotton, 126; selecting, 50–52
segregation, 153, 182–83, 204
Selective Service laws, 116
"Sentimental Journey," 82
sharecropping, 26
shaving, 117, 210
Shine (hand), 30, 43–45, 47, 48, 49, 64, 66, 85, 87, 88, 112
shoeshines, 117
shucking, 62–63
sickness: treating, 93–94, 208–209
sins: absolution of, 216
Skrabanek, Clara, 116–20, 122
Skrabanek, Ella, 107–11, 118, 213
Skrabanek, Henry, 101–107, 112, 213
Skrabanek, Johnnie, 120, 139, 169; memories of, 111–16; pranks of, 108–109, 112–13, 157, 162–63
Skrabanek, Robert L., photograph of, 5
Skrabanek family, photograph of, 6
Skrabanek house, 150–52
slot machines, 111
Slovacek, Josef, 10
smoking, 125
snacking, 174–75
Snook, John S., 14
Snook, Texas, 3–4, 10–11; Czech Moravian Brethren Church in, 77, 193; establishment of, 9–10; farming and, 16–17; naming of, 14; photographs of, 15, 34, 51, 142, 226; present-day, 225–29; schools in, 153
"The Snook Polka Boys," 130
Snowball (dog): poisoning of, 40
soda waters, 72, 111, 126, 174

Soil Conservation Program, 68
Sonny Boy, 104
spelling contests, 184
SPJST, 27, 77; committee, 78; establishment of, 11; hall, 128, 129, 151; loans from, 11, 26
sports, 105, 113–14, 185, 189, 229
"Stardust," 82
stewardship, 220
straight razor, 210. *See also* shaving
Student Czech Club, 191
suckers, 59–60
"Sugar Blues," 82
Sunday activities, 209–10, 213–14, 218–19
Sunday school, 213–15; attending, 203; description of, 211–12; preparing for, 204, 209–11

taroky (game), 98, 147
Taylor, Texas: dance at, 130
teachers, 154–55, 159
Texas A&M University, 107. *See also* Agricultural and Mechanical College of Texas
"Tex-Czech," 189
Tex-Mex, 189
Thanksgiving, 203
tithing, 220
Tobe (mule), 30
toilets, 186
"Toot Toot Tootsie, Good-bye," 82
track, 173–74
trapping, 40

Uncle Frank, 136–37
Uncle Joe, 137

Uncle John, 135
uncles: relationships with, 135–38
Unity of the Brethren, 193; beliefs of, 216–17
University of Texas, 106, 107
"Up a Lazy River," 82, 129
U.S. Army, 116
U.S. Navy, 116, 121

Valentino, Rudolph, 144
Vallee, Rudy, 130
vegetables: canning, 23; growing, 22–25; selling, 33

Washington County, 140
water: for hired hands, 66–67, 71; for school, 157–58, 167, 169
water fountains, 186
water system, 168, 181
Watkins Company, 94
Webster's dictionary, 153
weddings. *See* marriage
weeds, 7–8, 47
weevils, 52, 54, 61
Wesley, Texas: Brethren in, 193
WFAA (Dallas), 81
"Where Is My Home?" 9, 14
whippings, 169. *See also* punishment
wine making, 99–100
wood, 48–49
work. *See* farm work
work ethic, 76–77
workstock, 148; caring for, 31; types of, 29–30
World War II, 116, 143, 225
WPA, 66, 68–69

XERA (Mexico), 81

We're Czechs was composed into type in eleven point Palatino with two points of spacing between the lines. Condensed Palatino Italic was selected for display. The book was designed by Jim Billingsley, typeset by Metricomp, Inc., printed offset by Thomson-Shore, Inc., and bound by John H. Dekker & Sons. The paper on which the book is printed bears acid-free characteristics for an effective life of at least three hundred years.

TEXAS A&M UNIVERSITY PRESS : COLLEGE STATION